前言

自2009年国家汉办推出了新汉语水平考试（HSK）以来，HSK考生急剧增多。2012年全球HSK考生人数达到31万人，2013年第一季度已达7万人左右。随着汉语国际教育学科的不断壮大、海外孔子学院的不断增加，可以预计未来参加HSK考试的人员会越来越多。面对这样一个庞大的群体，如何引导他们有效地学习汉语，使他们在学习的过程中既能全方位地提高汉语综合运用能力，又能在HSK考试中取得理想成绩，一直是我们思考和研究的问题。编写一套以HSK大纲为纲，体现“考教结合”、“以考促教”、“以考促学”特点的新型汉语系列教材应当可以满足这一需求。在国家汉办考试处和北京语言大学出版社的指导下，我们结合多年的双语教学经验和对汉语水平考试的研究心得，研发了这套新型的考教结合系列教材《HSK标准教程》系列（以下简称“教程”）。

一、编写理念

进入21世纪，第二语言教学的理念已经进入后方法时代，以人为本，强调小组学习、合作学习，交际法、任务型语言教学、主题式教学成为教学的主流，培养学习者的语言综合运用能力成为教学的总目标。在这样一些理念的指导下，“教程”在编写过程中体现了以下特点：

1．以学生为中心，注重培养学生的听说读写综合运用能力

“考教结合”的前提是为学生的考试服务，但是仅仅为了考试就会走到应试的路子上去，这不是我们编教的初衷。如何在为考试服务的前提下重点提高学生的语言能力是我们一直在探索的问题，也是本套教材的特色之一。以HSK一、二级为例，这两级的考试只涉及听力和阅读，不涉及说和写，但是在教材中我们从一级开始就进行有针对性的语音和汉字的学习和练习，并且吸收听说法和认知法的长处，课文以“情景+对话+图片”为主，训练学生的听说技能。练习册重点训练学生的听力、阅读和写的技能，综合起来培养学生的听说读写能力。

2．融入交际法和任务型语言教学的核心理念

交际法强调语言表达的得体性和语境的作用，任务型语言教学强调语言的真实性和在完成一系列任务的过程中学习语言，两种教学法都强调语言的真实和情境的设置，以及在交际过程中培养学生的语言能力。HSK考试不是以哪一本教材为依据进行的成绩测试，而是依据汉语水平考试大纲而制定的，是考查学习者语言能力的能力测试。基于这样的认识，“教程”编写就不能像以往教材那样，以语言点为核心进行举一反三式的重复和训练，这样就不能应对考试涉及的方方面面的内容，因此我们在保证词语和语法点不超纲的前提下，采取变换情境的方式，让学习者体会在不同情境下语言的真实运用，在模拟和真实体验中学习和习得汉语。

3．体现了主题式教学的理念

主题式教学是以内容为载体、以文本的内涵为主体所进行的一种语言教学活动，它强调内容的多样性和丰富性，一般来说，一个主题确定后，通过接触和这个主题相关的多个方面的学习内容，加速学生对新内容的内化和理解，进而深入探究，培养学生的创造能力。“教程”为了联系学生的实际，开阔学生的视野，从四级分册开始以主题引领，每个主题下又分为若干小主题，主题之间相互联系形成有机的知识网络，使之牢固地镶嵌在学生的记忆深处，不易遗忘。

二、“教程”的特色

1．以汉语水平考试大纲为依据，逐级编写“教程”

汉语水平考试（HSK）共分六个等级，“教程”编教人员仔细研读了“大纲”和出题指南，并对大量真题进行了统计、分析。根据真题统计结果归纳出每册的重点、难点、语言点、话题、功能、场景等，在遵循HSK大纲词汇要求的前提下，系统设计了各级别的范围、课时等，具体安排如下：

教材分册	教学目标	词汇量（词）	教学时数（学时）
教程1	HSK（一级）	150	30–34
教程2	HSK（二级）	300	30–36
教程3	HSK（三级）	600	35–40
教程4（上/下）	HSK（四级）	1200	75–80
教程5（上/下）	HSK（五级）	2500	170–180
教程6（上/下）	HSK（六级）	5000 及以上	170–180
总计：9册		5000 以上	510–550

这种设计遵循汉语国际教育的理念，注重教材的普适性、应用性和实用性，海内外教学机构可根据学时建议来设计每册书完成的年限。比如，一级的《教程1》规定用34学时完成，如果国内周课时是8课时的话，大概一个月左右就能学完；在海外如果一周是4课时的话，就需要两个月的时间能学完。以此类推。一般来说，学完《教程1》就能通过一级考试，同样学完《教程2》就能通过二级考试，等等。

2．每册教材配有练习册，练习册中练习的形式与HSK题型吻合

为了使学习者适应HSK的考试题型，教材的各级练习册设计的练习题型均与HSK考试题型吻合，从练习的顺序到练习的结构等都与考题试卷保持一致，练习的内容以本课的内容为主，目的是学习者学完教材就能适应HSK考试，不需额外熟悉考试形式。

3．单独设置交际练习，紧密结合HSK口试内容

在HSK考试中，口试独立于笔试之外，为了培养学生的口语表达能力，在教程中，每一课都提供交际练习，包括双人活动和小组活动等，为学习者参加口试提供保障。

本套教程在策划和研发过程中得到了孔子学院总部/国家汉办、北京语言大学出版社和汉考国际（CTI）的大力支持和指导，是全体编者与出版社总编、编辑和汉办考试处、汉考国际命题研发人员集体智慧的结晶。本人代表编写组对以上机构和各位参与者表示衷心的感谢！我们希望使用本教程的师生，能够毫无保留地把使用的意见和建议反馈给我们，以便进一步完善，使其成为教师好教、学生好学、教学好用的好教程。

姜丽萍

2013年11月

本册说明

《HSK标准教程1》适合未系统学习过汉语的零起点学习者以及准备参加HSK（一级）考试的汉语学习者使用。

一、全书共15课，除第1课、第2课以语音为主外，从第3课开始每课围绕一个主题，分3个场景，每个场景1~2个话轮安排对话，每课10~15个生词，3~4个语言点注释。一级教程编写严格遵循HSK（一级）大纲规定的150词，本册教程只有10个超纲词（在书中用“*”标识），而且这些超纲词都是二、三级词语。每课建议授课时间为2~3学时。

二、第1课、第2课是语音学习的入门阶段，系统介绍汉语的声母、韵母、声调、音节结构等语音基本知识，目的在于使学习者全面了解并掌握汉语的基本语音面貌，为后面进一步学习打下良好的语音基础，因此发音示范、正音、纠音是教学的重点和难点。本书语音部分以图文并茂的形式介绍语音，力求使学习者在入门阶段就把音和义结合起来，提高学习兴趣。本部分除了语音知识的介绍以外，课文部分还给出了打招呼、告别、致谢、道歉等常用的简短表达方式，教学时建议把语音练习和交际练习结合起来。

三、第3课到第15课每课设置热身、课文（含生词）、注释、练习、拼音、汉字、运用七个部分；每5课设置一个文化板块，以介绍相关的文化背景知识为主。

1．**热身**。热身部分主要使用图片进行本课重点词语、短语的导入，教师可以根据教学需要安排学习者对热身部分的内容提前预习，充分调动学习者的学习积极性，课上教师在使用这部分的图片和文字内容时方法可不拘一格，目的是以直观的形式帮助学习者进行新知识的学习，提高学习者的学习兴趣和效率。

2．**课文**。每课课文包含三个不同的情景，每个情景有1~2个话轮。与传统教材针对一段内容反复操练重点句型和生词的形式不同，本教材以大纲中的词语为重点，将词语与HSK（一级）考试真题句编入课文对话中，并在不同情景下进行复现。这样的设计既能帮助学习者熟悉语言真实的使用环境，又能引导学习者适应快速的情景转换，为HSK（一级）考试中的听力和阅读部分打好基础。

3．**注释**。本教程弱化语法，语言点讲解采用注释的方式，多用表格形式展示，力求简洁、清楚、易学易懂。每个语法项目的解释只涉及本课课文中的用法，并从易到难搭配例句，其中变颜色的例句为该语言点在课文中的原句。采用注释的方式处理语言点，一方面希望减少零起点汉语初学者的学习压力和畏难情绪，另一方面也贯彻了本教材以练代讲、多练少讲的原则。

4．**练习**。练习环节安排在每课语言点注释之后。练习的内容为本课新学的语言点和重点词语，目的是使当天学习的内容得到及时强化，并训练学生的听说能力和语言交际能力。练习形式主要有回答问题、图片描述、完成句子等，这些练习形式也与HSKK初级口语考试题型相吻合，也在为学习者的口语考试做铺垫。练习采用比较直观的方式，这个环节教师可以灵活安排，可以在课文讲练之后使用，也可以在语法解释之后使用，更可以在本课小结时用来检测学习者的学习情况。

5. **拼音**。语音部分第3课到第5课主要介绍声母、韵母重点和难点音的发音辨析，教学时建议以语音训练为主，不必逐词讲解词义，学习者能够掌握正确的发音即可。第6课到第15课主要介绍双音节词语、三音节词语以及含有轻声音节词语的声调搭配，其中，双音节词语的声调搭配是教学重点。每个双音节词语的声调模式都给出了一个标准词并配图片作为学习者模仿记忆的范本，力求使之成为以后其他词语声调模式的发音参照。

6. **汉字**。汉字教学内容为17个笔画，6个笔顺，7个汉字结构，52个独体字和18个偏旁。独体字教学贯穿汉字教学的始终，通过对前三级的600个词进行统计，选出其中最常用、构字能力最强的52个独体字进入一级教学中。第1课到第6课介绍基本笔画，从第7课开始进行偏旁教学，每课介绍两个易学、常见、构字能力强的偏旁，并给出两个例字。一级汉字主要进行认读的训练，只对17个基本笔画和52个独体字有书写要求。

7. **运用**。一级主要设计有互动性强的双人活动和交际性强的小组活动，以提高学生的汉语综合运用能力。

8. **文化**。一级共安排三个文化点，分布在第5课、第10课和第15课。针对本级别的学习者所选取的文化点主要是日常生活交往方面的交际性文化。三个文化点分别为：中国人对年龄的询问方法，中国人姓名的特点，中国人经常使用的通信工具。建议教师结合该部分的图片和内容，引入一些中国文化的探讨和交流内容，可以使用媒介语。

以上是对本教材课本教程使用方法的一些说明和建议。在教学过程中您可以根据实际情况灵活使用本教材。对于零起点汉语学习者来说，这是他们学习汉语的入门教材。我们希望打破汉语很难的印象，让学习者学得快乐、学得轻松、学得高效。学完本书，就可以通过HSK相应级别的考试来检测自己的能力和水平。希望本教材可以帮助每位学习者在学习汉语的道路上开个好头并走得更远。

目录 Contents

拼音 *Pinyin*	汉字 Characters
1. 汉语拼音的声母和韵母（1）： Initials and Finals of Chinese *Pinyin* (1): b、p、m、f、d、t、n、l、g、k、h、j、q、x i、u、ü、er、a、ia、ua、o、uo、e、ie、üe、ai、uai、ei、uei (ui)、ao、iao 2. 汉语的声调（四声）Tones (Four Tones) 3. 汉语的音节 Chinese Syllables 4. 两个三声音节的连读变调 Tone Sandhi: 3rd tone + 3rd tone	1. 汉字的笔画（1）： Strokes of Chinese Characters (1): 一、丨、丿、丶、㇏ 2. 认识独体字：Single-Component Characters: 一、二、三、十、八、六
1. 汉语拼音的声母和韵母（2）： Initials and Finals of Chinese *Pinyin* (2): zh、ch、sh、r、z、c、s ou、iou (iu)、an、ian、uan、üan、en、in、uen (un)、ün、ang、iang、uang、eng、ing、ueng、ong、iong 2. 汉语的轻声 The Neutral Tone 3. 拼音规则（1）：标调法和省写 Rules of *Pinyin* (1): Tone Marking and Abbreviation	1. 汉字的笔画（2）： Strokes of Chinese Characters (2): ㇇、㇄、亅 2. 认识独体字：Single-Component Characters: 口、见、山、小、不
1. 发音辨析：声母j、q、x和z、c、s Differentiation: pronunciation of the initials j, q, x and z, c, s 2. 发音辨析：韵母i、u、ü Differentiation: pronunciation of the finals i, u, ü 3. "不"的变调 Tone Sandhi of "不 (bù)" 4. 拼音规则（2）：单韵母 ü 和 ü 开头的韵母跟 j、q、x 相拼的规则 Rules of *Pinyin* (2): ü or finals led by ü with j, q, x	1. 汉字的笔画（3）： Strokes of Chinese Characters (3): ㇆、㇃ 2. 认识独体字：Single-Component Characters: 月、心、中、人 3. 汉字的笔顺（1）：先横后竖，先撇后捺 Stroke Order (1): horizontal preceding vertical and left-falling preceding right-falling
1. 发音辨析：声母zh、ch、sh、r Differentiation: pronunciation of the initials zh, ch, sh, r 2. 发音辨析：前鼻音韵母n和后鼻音韵母ng Differentiation: pronunciation of the alveolar nasal n and the velar nasal ng 3. "一"的变调 Tone Sandhi of "一 (yī)" 4. 拼音规则（3）：y、w 的用法 Rules of *Pinyin* (3): use of y and w	1. 汉字的笔画（4）： Strokes of Chinese Characters (4): ㇗、㇠ 2. 认识独体字：Single-Component Characters: 七、儿、几、九 3. 汉字的笔顺（2）：从上到下，从左到右 Stroke Order (2): top preceding bottom and left preceding right
1. 儿化的发音 The Retroflex Final 2. 发音辨析：以i、u、ü开头的韵母 Differentiation: pronunciation of finals beginning with i, u, ü 3. 声母送气音和不送气音发音的区别 Difference between Aspirated and Unaspirated Initials 4. 拼音规则（4）：隔音符号 Rules of *Pinyin* (4): syllable-dividing mark	1. 汉字的笔画（5）： Strokes of Chinese Characters (5): ㇇、㇛ 2. 认识独体字：Single-Component Characters: 水、女、了、大 3. 汉字的笔顺（3）：先外后内，先中间后两边 Stroke Order (3): outside preceding inside and middle preceding sides

拼音 *Pinyin*	汉字 Characters
双音节词语的声调搭配（1）：一声和各声调的搭配 Tone Collocation in Disyllabic Words (1): 1st tone + 1st/2nd/3rd/4th tone	1. 汉字的笔画（6）： Strokes of Chinese Characters (6): 𠃋、㇂、㇀ 2. 认识独体字：Single-Component Characters: 东、我、西 3. 汉字结构（1）：独体结构与合体结构 Structure of Chinese Characters (1): single-component and compound
双音节词语的声调搭配（2）：二声和各声调的搭配 Tone Collocation in Disyllabic Words (2): 2nd tone + 1st/2nd/3rd/4th tone	1. 认识独体字：Single-Component Characters: 四、五、书 2. 汉字结构（2）：左右结构与左中右结构 Structure of Chinese Characters (2): left-right and left-middle-right 3. 汉字偏旁“氵”和“讠” Chinese Radicals: “氵” and “讠”
双音节词语的声调搭配（3）：三声和各声调的搭配 Tone Collocation in Disyllabic Words (3): 3rd tone + 1st/2nd/3rd/4th tone	1. 认识独体字：Single-Component Characters: 少、个 2. 汉字结构（3）：上下结构与上中下结构 Structure of Chinese Characters (3): top-bottom and top-middle-bottom 3. 汉字偏旁“钅”和“口” Chinese Radicals: “钅” and “口”
双音节词语的声调搭配（4）：四声和各声调的搭配 Tone Collocation in Disyllabic Words (4): 4th tone + 1st/2nd/3rd/4th tone	1. 认识独体字：Single-Component Characters: 在、子、工 2. 汉字结构（4）：半包围结构 Structure of Chinese Characters (4): half-enclosure 3. 汉字偏旁“辶”和“门” Chinese Radicals: “辶” and “门”
1. 轻声音节的读法 Pronunciation of Neutral-Tone Syllables 2. 叠音词的读法 Pronunciation of Reduplicated Syllables 3. 带后缀词的读法：“-们，-子，-头” Pronunciation of Words with the Suffix “-们”, “-子” or “-头”	1. 认识独体字：Single-Component Characters: 上、下、本、末 2. 汉字结构（5）：全包围结构 Structure of Chinese Characters (5): enclosure 3. 汉字偏旁“口”和“礻” Chinese Radicals: “口” and “礻”

拼音 *Pinyin*	汉字 Characters
轻声的功能 Function of Neutral-Tone Syllables	1. 认识独体字：Single-Component Characters: 午、电 2. 汉字偏旁“阝”和“亻” Chinese Radicals: “阝” and “亻”
三音节词语的声调搭配（1）：一声音节开头 Tone Collocation in Trisyllabic Words (1): words starting with a first-tone syllable	1. 认识独体字：Single-Component Characters: 天、气、雨 2. 汉字偏旁“女”和“饣” Chinese Radicals: “女” and “饣”
三音节词语的声调搭配（2）：二声音节开头 Tone Collocation in Trisyllabic Words (2): words starting with a second-tone syllable	1. 认识独体字：Single-Component Characters: 日、目、习 2. 汉字偏旁“日”和“目” The Chinese Radicals: “日” and “目”
三音节词语的声调搭配（3）：三声音节开头 Tone Collocation in Trisyllabic Words (3): words starting with a third-tone syllable	1. 认识独体字：Single-Component Characters 开、车、回 2. 汉字偏旁“月”和“扌” Chinese Radicals: “月” and “扌”
三音节词语的声调搭配（4）：四声音节开头 Tone Collocation in Trisyllabic Words (4): words starting with a fourth-tone syllable	1. 认识独体字：Single-Component Characters: 年、出、飞 2. 汉字偏旁“艹”和“宀” Chinese Radicals: “艹” and “宀”

1

Nǐ hǎo
你好
Hello

课文 Text

1 01-1

Nǐ hǎo!
A: 你好！

Nǐ hǎo!
B: 你好！

English Version

A: Hello!

B: Hello!

New Words

1. 你 nǐ pron. (*singular*) you
2. 好 hǎo adj. good, fine

2 01-2

Nín hǎo!
A: 您 好！

Nǐmen hǎo!
B: 你们 好！

English Version

A: Hello!

B: Hello!

New Words

*3. 您 nín pron. (*polite*) you

4. 你们 nǐmen pron. (*plural*) you

3 01-3

Duìbuqǐ!
A: 对不起！

Méi guānxi!
B: 没 关系！

English Version

A: I'm sorry!

B: That's OK!

New Words

5. 对不起 duìbuqǐ v. to be sorry
6. 没关系 méi guānxi that's OK, it doesn't matter

拼音 Pinyin

1 汉语拼音的声母和韵母（1） Initials and Finals of Chinese *Pinyin* (1) 01-4

声母 Initials（1）				韵母 Finals（1）			
b	p	m	f	i	u	ü	er
d	t	n	l	ɑ	iɑ	uɑ	
g	k	h		o	uo		
j	q	x		e	ie	üe	
				ɑi	uɑi		
				ei	uei (ui)		
				ɑo	iɑo		

2 汉语的声调（四声） Tones (Four Tones)

汉语的基本声调有四个，分别是第一声（55）、第二声（35）、第三声（214）和第四声（51）。汉语的声调有区别意义的作用。

There are four basic tones in Chinese, respectively called the 1st tone (55), the 2nd tone (35), the 3rd tone (214) and the 4th tone (51). They make difference in meaning.

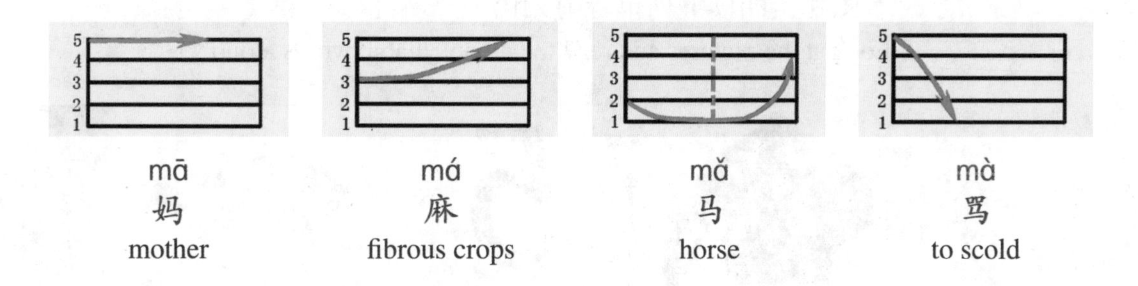

mā	má	mǎ	mà
妈	麻	马	骂
mother	fibrous crops	horse	to scold

朗读下列音节，注意声调的不同 01-5

Read the syllables aloud and pay attention to the tones.

ā	á	ǎ	à
ō	ó	ǒ	ò
ē	é	ě	è
ī	í	ǐ	ì
ū	ú	ǔ	ù
ǖ	ǘ	ǚ	ǜ

3 汉语的音节 Chinese Syllables

汉语的音节一般由声母、韵母、声调三部分组成。一般来说，一个汉字对应一个音节。汉语的一个音节可以没有声母，但是一定要有韵母和声调。

A Chinese syllable is usually made up of an initial, a final and a tone. Generally speaking, one Chinese character corresponds to one syllable. A Chinese syllable can have no initial, but must have a final and a tone.

汉语的音节 Syllable	声母 Initial	韵母 Final	声调 Tone
māo（猫，cat）	m	ao	ˉ
yú （鱼，fish）		ü	ˊ
jiě （姐，elder sister）	j	ie	ˇ
èr （二，two）		er	ˋ

*注意：i和ü自成音节时，韵母前增加y，ü上的两点去掉；u自成音节时，韵母前增加w。

Note: When *i* or *ü* acts as a syllable by itself, *y* is added before it, with the two dots on the top of *ü* being removed; when *u* acts as a syllable by itself, *w* is added before it.

看图片，朗读下列双音节词语 01-7

Look at the pictures and read the disyllabic words aloud.

4 两个三声音节的连读变调 Tone Sandhi: 3rd tone + 3rd tone

当两个第三声音节连读时，第一个音节变为第二声，3 + 3 变为 2 + 3。比如“nǐ（你）” + “hǎo（好）” 变为 “ní hǎo” 。但是注音时，要标原调。

When two third-tone syllables are read in sequence, the first syllable turns into the second tone, i.e., the 3+3 sequence becomes a 2+3 one. For example, “nǐ（你）” + “hǎo（好）” is read “ní hǎo”. However, when put in the written form, the original tone is kept.

ˇ +	ˇ →	ˊ +	ˇ
nǐ（你）	hǎo（好）	ní	hǎo
kě（可）	yǐ（以）	ké	yǐ
fǔ（辅）	dǎo（导）	fú	dǎo

朗读下列词语，注意第三声音节的读音 01-8

Read the following words aloud and pay attention to the change in the tone of the 3rd tone syllables.

nǐ hǎo	kěyǐ	fǔdǎo	xiǎojiě
kǒuyǔ	yǔfǎ	Fǎyǔ	tǎo hǎo
liǎojiě	yǒuhǎo	yǔsǎn	shǒubiǎo

课堂用语 Classroom Expressions

01-9

上课！	Shàng kè!	Class begins!
下课！	Xià kè!	Class is over!
现在休息！	Xiànzài xiūxi!	Take a break now!
看黑板！	Kàn hēibǎn!	Look at the blackboard!
跟我读！	Gēn wǒ dú!	Read after me!

汉字 Characters

1 汉字的笔画（1）：一、丨、丿、丶、㇏

Strokes of Chinese Characters (1): 一, 丨, 丿, 丶, ㇏

笔画名称 Stroke	运笔方向 Direction	例字 Example Characters
一 横 héng horizontal		一 yī one 二 èr two
丨 竖 shù vertical		十 shí ten 工 gōng work, labor
丿 撇 piě left-falling		人 rén human 八 bā eight
丶 点 diǎn dot		不 bù no, not 六 liù six
㇏ 捺 nà right-falling		大 dà big 天 tiān sky

2 认识独体字 Single-Component Characters

（1）“一”，是汉字的基本笔画，也可单独成为汉字表示数量“1”。

“一” is one of the basic strokes of Chinese characters. The single-component character “一” means “one”.

yī

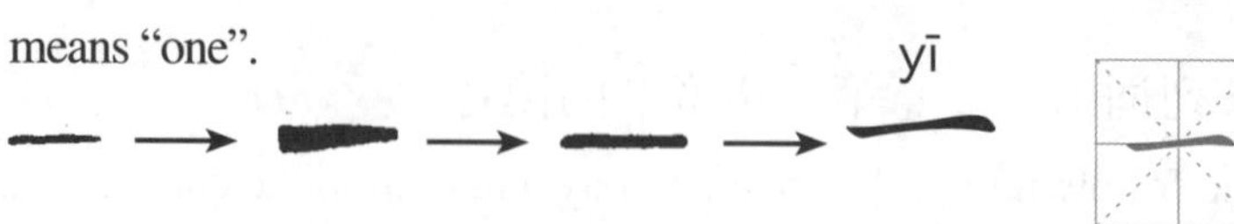

（2）“二”，表示数量“2”。

“二” means “two”.

èr

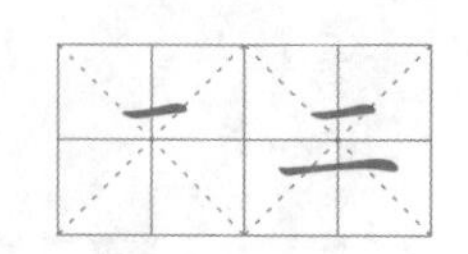

（3）“三”，表示数量“3”。

“三” means “three”.

sān

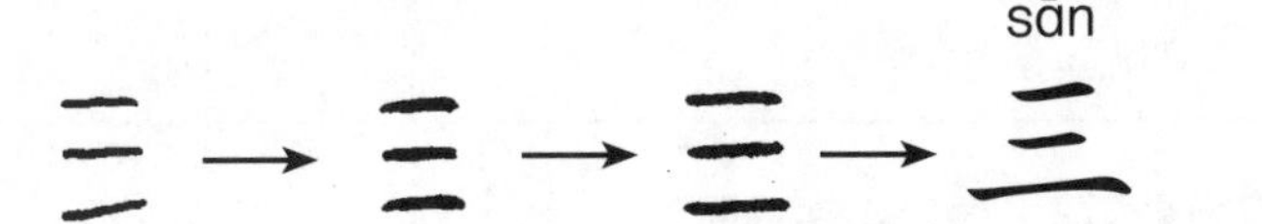

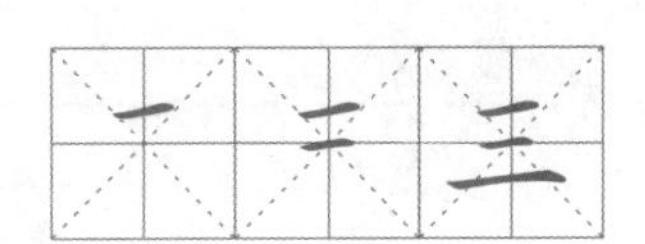

（4）“十”，表示数量“10”。

“十” means “ten”.

shí

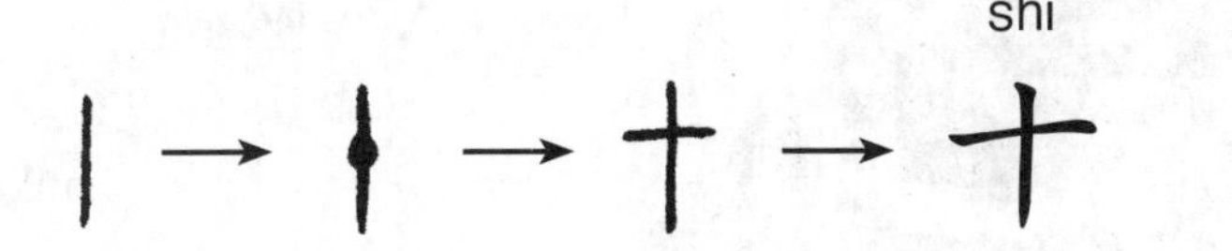

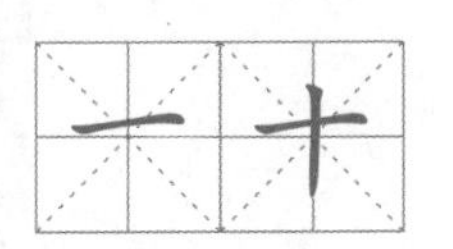

（5）“八”，表示数量“8”。

“八” means “eight”.

bā

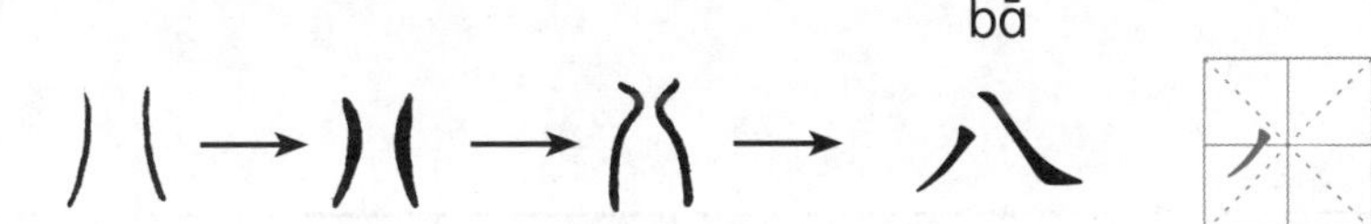

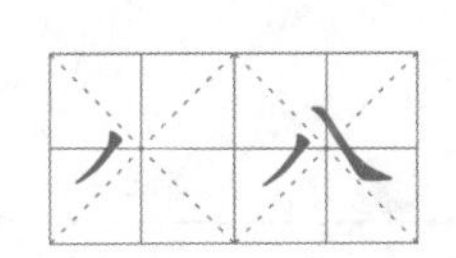

（6）“六”，表示数量“6”。

“六” means “six”.

liù

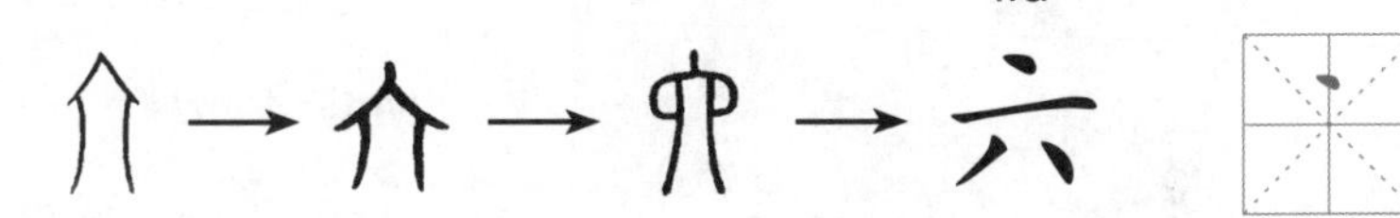

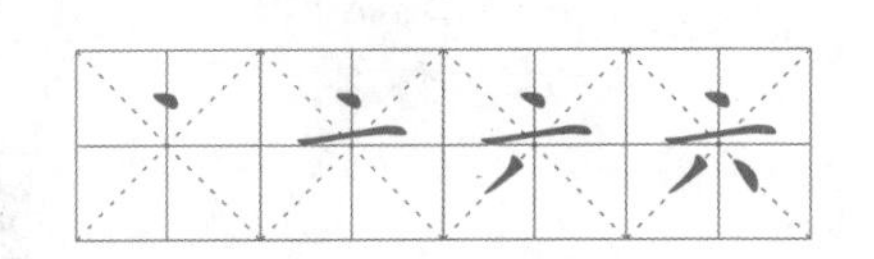

2 Xièxie nǐ 谢谢你 Thank you

课文 Text

1 02-1

Xièxie!
A: 谢谢!

Bú xiè!
B: 不谢!

English Version

A: Thank you!
B: Sure!

New Words

1. 谢谢 xièxie v. to thank
2. 不 bù adv. no, not

2 02-2

Xièxie nǐ!
A: 谢谢你!

Bú kèqi!
B: 不客气!

English Version

A: Thank you!
B: You're welcome!

New Word

3. 不客气 bú kèqi you're welcome, don't mention it

3 02-3

Zàijiàn!
A: 再见!

Zàijiàn!
B: 再见!

English Version

A: Goodbye!
B: Bye!

New Word

4. 再见 zàijiàn v. to see you around

拼音 Pinyin

1 汉语拼音的声母和韵母（2） Initials and Finals of Chinese *Pinyin* (2)  02-4

声母 Initials（2）				韵母 Finals（2）			
zh	ch	sh	r	ou	iou (iu)		
z	c	s		an	ian	uan	üan
				en	in	uen (un)	ün
				ang	iang	uang	
				eng	ing	ueng	
				ong	iong		

看图片，朗读下列单音节词语 02-5

Look at the pictures and read the monosyllabic words aloud.

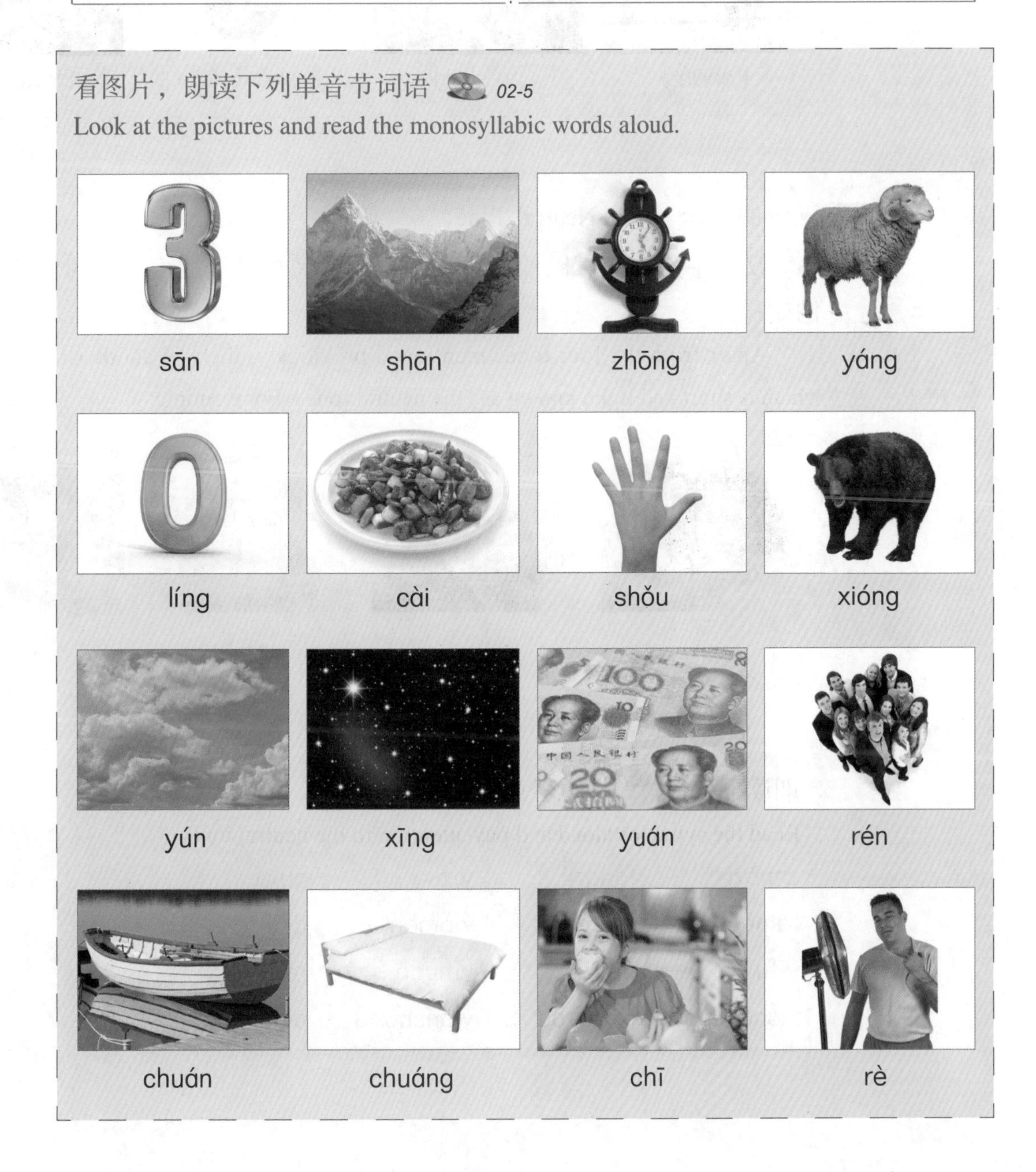

看图片，朗读下列双音节词语 02-6
Look at the pictures and read the disyllabic words aloud.

2 汉语的轻声 The Neutral Tone

汉语中除了四声以外，还有一个读得又短又轻的声调，叫作“轻声”。例如：

Apart from the four tones mentioned previously, there is another tone in Chinese, which is short and light, known as “the neutral tone”. For example:

朗读下列音节，注意轻声的读法 02-7
Read the syllables aloud and pay attention to the neutral tone.

zhuōzi	fángzi	yǐzi	guìzi
tāmen	rénmen	wǒmen	dìdi
yīfu	érzi	xǐhuan	rènshi
xiānsheng	péngyou	wǎnshang	piàoliang

3 拼音规则（1）：标调法和省写

Rules of *Pinyin* (1): Tone Marking and Abbreviation

（1）标调法 Tone Marking

汉语拼音的声调必须标注在元音字母上。当一个韵母含有两个或者两个以上元音字母时，调号标注在开口度较大的那个元音字母上。调号标注的主要元音顺序为 a、o、e、i、u、ü，但iu是个例外，iu 是 iou 的省略形式，声调标注在 u 上。轻声音节不标声调。

Tone marks in Chinese *pinyin* are put above vowels. When there are two or more vowels in the final of a syllable, the tone should be marked on the one that is pronounced with the mouth more wide-open, the sequence being "*a, o, e, i, u, ü*" in the descending order. The compound final *iu* is an exception to this rule, in which the tone mark is put on *u* rather than *i* as *iu* is the abbreviation of *iou*. The neutral tone is unmarked.

朗读下列音节，注意声调标注的位置 02-8

Read the syllables aloud and pay attention to the positions of the tone marks.

xuéxiào	bāng máng	lánqiú	nǚ'ér
yóu yǒng	shǒubiǎo	zhōngyú	gōngsī
shíjiān	shēntǐ	kǎoshì	guójiā
bàozhǐ	hǎochī	xièxie	kèqi

（2）省写 Abbreviation

iou、uei、uen 前面加声母的时候，写成：iu、ui、un。例如 niu、gui、lun。

When *iou*, *uei* or *uen* follows an initial, they are written as *iu*, *ui* and *un* respectively, for example, *niu*, *gui*, *lun*.

朗读下列音节，注意韵母省写的部分 02-9

Read the syllables aloud and pay attention to the abbreviated finals.

xiūxi	shuì jiào	lúnchuán	niúnǎi
píjiǔ	ángguì	liúyán	kāi huì
tǎolùn	zúqiú	Lúndūn	shīrùn
cánkuì	shuǐguǒ	táozuì	shùnlì

课堂用语 Classroom Expressions

02-10

打开书。	Dǎkāi shū.	Open your book.
请大声读。	Qǐng dà shēng dú.	Read aloud.
再读一遍。	Zài dú yí biàn.	Read once again. /Repeat.
一起读。	Yìqǐ dú.	Read together.
有问题吗？	Yǒu wèntí ma?	Any questions?

汉字 Characters

1 汉字的笔画（2）：㇆、𠃊、亅

Strokes of Chinese Characters (2): ㇆, 𠃊, 亅

笔画名称 Stroke	运笔方向 Direction	例字 Example Characters
㇆ 横折 héngzhé horizontal-turning		口 kǒu mouth 日 rì sun
𠃊 竖折 shùzhé vertical-turning		山 shān mountain 出 chū to come/go out
亅 竖钩 shùgōu vertical hook		丁 dīng man, member of a family 小 xiǎo small, little

2 认识独体字 Single-Component Characters

（1）“口”，本义是嘴巴，字形像人张开的嘴巴。

The basic meaning of “口” is “mouth”, and the character is shaped like a mouth.

kǒu

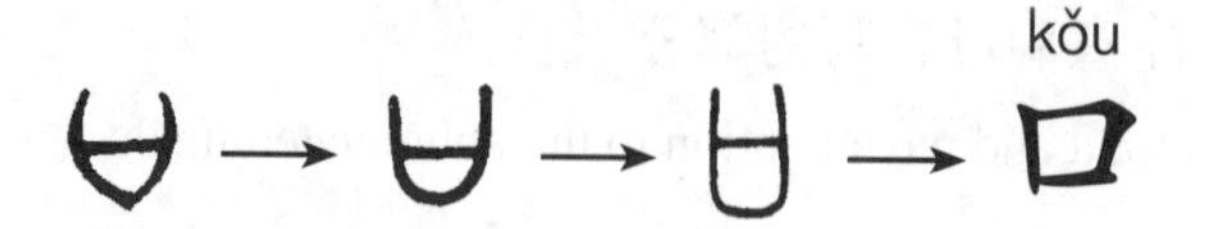

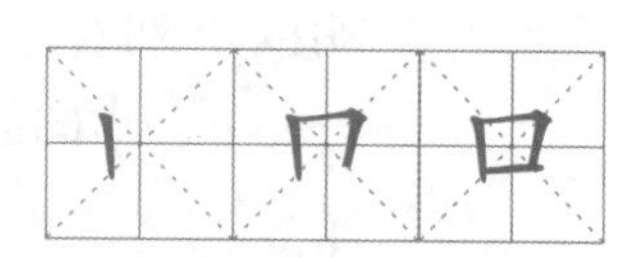

（2）“见”，字形上边是“目”，下边是“人”，意思是“睁着眼睛看”。

Its traditional form of “见” has a “目 (eye)” on the top and a “人 (person)” at the bottom, meaning “watching with eyes open”.

jiàn

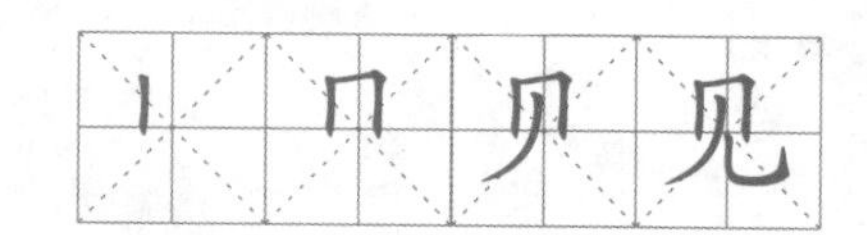

（3）“山”，字形像起伏的山峰，意思是“山峰”。

“山” means “mountain” and was originally shaped like rolling mountains.

shān

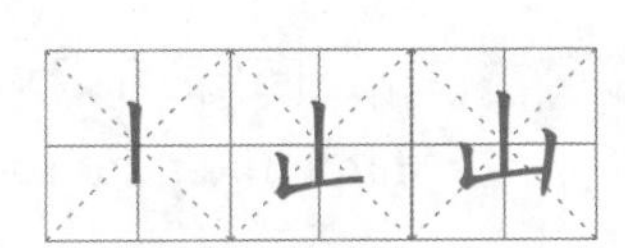

（4）“小”，字形像细微的沙，现在意思与“大”相对。

“小” was originally shaped like tiny grains of sand. Now it means “small”, opposite to “大 (big)”.

xiǎo

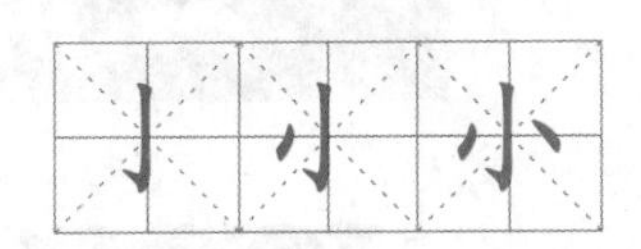

（5）“不”，原来表示一种工具，现在虚化为副词，表示否定。

“不” originally referred to a tool. Now it's a negative adverb.

bù

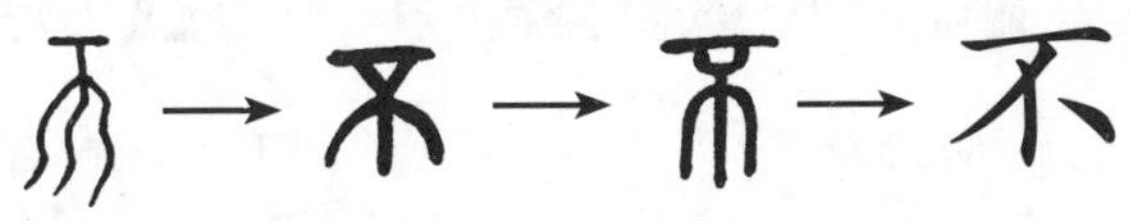

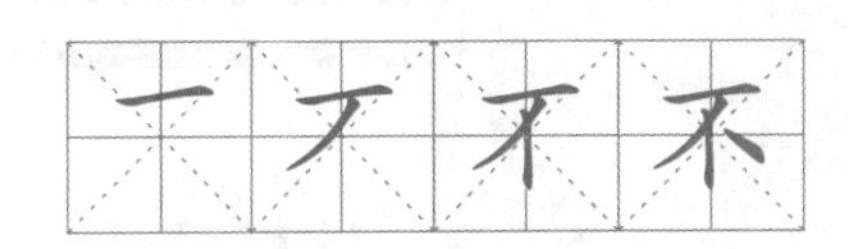

3 Nǐ jiào shénme míngzi
你叫什么名字
What's your name

热身 Warm-up

给下面的词语选择对应的图片

Match the pictures with the words/phrases.

Zhōngguó ① 中国 ________	Měiguó ② 美国 ________	Zhōngguó rén ③ 中国 人 ________
Měiguó rén ④ 美国 人 ________	lǎoshī ⑤ 老师 ________	xuésheng ⑥ 学生 ________

课文 Text

1 在学校 In the school 03-1

Nǐ jiào shénme míngzi?

A: 你叫 什么 名字?

Wǒ jiào Lǐ Yuè.

B: 我 叫 李 月。

English Version

A: What's your name?

B: My name is Li Yue.

New Words

1. 叫 jiào v. to call, to be called
2. 什么 shénme pron. what
3. 名字 míngzi n. name
4. 我 wǒ pron. I, me

Proper Noun

1. 李月 Lǐ Yuè Li Yue, name of a person

2 在教室 In the classroom 03-2

Nǐ shì lǎoshī ma?

A: 你是老师吗?

Wǒ bú shì lǎoshī, wǒ shì xuésheng.

B: 我不是老师，我是学生。

English Version

A: Are you a teacher?

B: No, I'm not. I'm a student.

New Words

5. 是 shì v. to be
6. 老师 lǎoshī n. teacher
7. 吗 ma part. *used at the end of a question*
8. 学生 xuésheng n. student

3 在学校 In the school 03-3

Nǐ shì Zhōngguó rén ma?

A: 你是中国人吗?

Wǒ bú shì Zhōngguó rén, wǒ shì Měiguó rén.

B: 我不是中国人，我是美国人。

English Version

A: Are you Chinese?

B: No, I'm not. I'm American.

New Word

9. 人 rén n. human, person

Proper Nouns

2. 中国 Zhōngguó China
3. 美国 Měiguó the United States of America

注释 Notes

1 疑问代词“什么” The Interrogative Pronoun “什么”

疑问代词“什么”表示疑问，用在疑问句中可直接做宾语，或者与后接名词性成分一起做宾语。例如:

The interrogative pronoun “什么” is used in interrogative sentences, serving as the object by itself or together with a nominal element following it. For example:

（1）你叫什么名字?

（2）这（zhè，this）是什么?

（3）这（zhè，this）是什么书（shū，book）?

2 “是”字句 The “是” Sentence

“是”字句是由“是”构成的判断句，用于表达人或事物等于什么或者属于什么。其否定形式是在“是”前加上否定副词“不”。例如：

A “是” sentence is a determinative sentence with “是”, indicating what somebody or something equals or belongs to. The negative sentence is formed by adding the negative adverb “不” before “是”. For example:

Subject	Predicate	
	（不）是	Noun/Noun Phrase
李月	是	老师。
我	是	美国人。
我	不是	老师。

3 用“吗”的疑问句 Interrogative Sentences with “吗”

疑问助词“吗”表示疑问语气，用在陈述句句尾构成疑问句。例如：

The particle “吗” indicates an interrogative mood. When “吗” is added at the end of a declarative sentence, the declarative sentence turns into a question. For example:

Subject	Predicate		
	Verb	Noun/Noun Phrase	吗?
你	是	美国人	吗?
你	是	中国人	吗?
你	是	老师	吗?

练习 Exercises

1 分角色朗读课文 Role-play the dialogues.

2 根据实际情况回答问题 Answer the questions according to the actual situations.

1. 你叫什么名字? Nǐ jiào shénme míngzi?
2. 你是中国人吗? Nǐ shì Zhōngguó rén ma?
3. 你是美国人吗? Nǐ shì Měiguó rén ma?
4. 你是老师吗? Nǐ shì lǎoshī ma?
5. 你是学生吗? Nǐ shì xuésheng ma?

3 用本课新学的语言点和词语描述图片

Describe the pictures using the newly-learned language points and words.

Tā jiào Qiáodān, tā shì rén.
他叫 乔丹 (Michael Jordan)，他是________人。

Tā jiào Yáo Míng, tā shì rén.
他叫 姚 明 (Yao Ming)，他是________人。

Wǒ bú shì wǒ shì xuésheng, wǒ shì rén.
我不是________，我是 学生，我是________人。

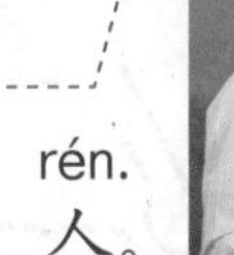

Wǒ shì wǒ bú shì xuésheng, wǒ shì rén.
我是________，我不是 学生，我是________人。

拼音 Pinyin

1 发音辨析：声母j、q、x和z、c、s

Differentiation: pronunciation of the initials j, q, x and z, c, s

j、q、x是舌面音，发j、q时舌面要与硬腭接触，j没有强烈的气流呼出，而q有强烈的气流呼出。发x时，舌面接近硬腭，但不要接触，始终保持一条缝隙。

j, *q* and *x* are known as coronals. The surface of the tongue touches the hard palate when pronouncing *j* and *q*. While *q* brings out a strong airflow, *j* doesn't. When *x* is pronounced, the surface of the tongue approaches the hard palate without reaching it, leaving a gap in between.

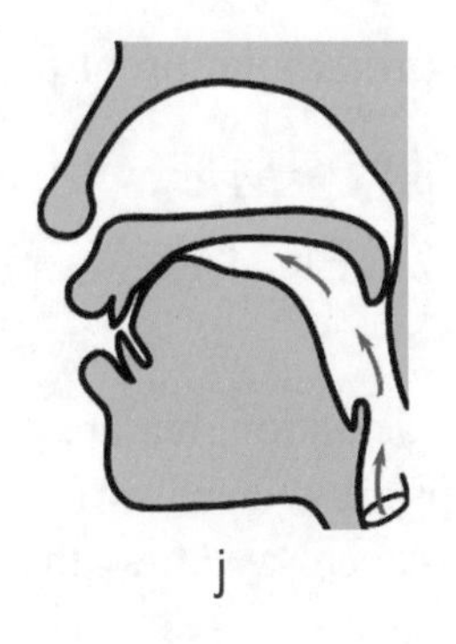
j

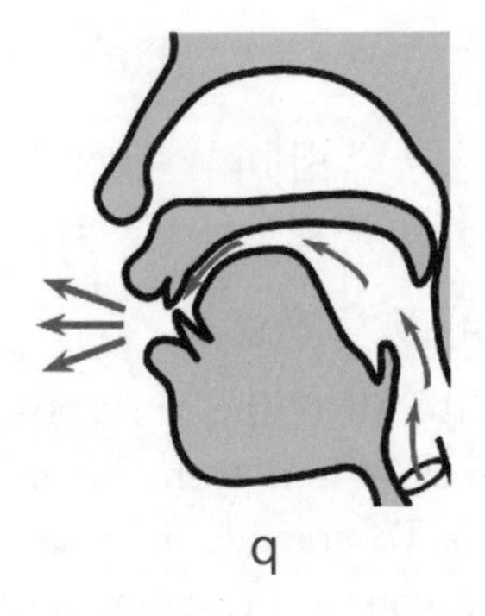
q

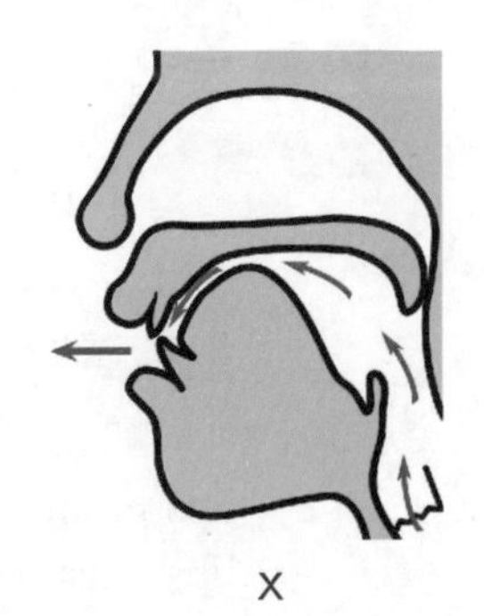
x

听录音并跟读，注意声母发音的区别 03-4

Listen to the recording and read after it. Pay attention to the differences between the initials.

xiūxi	jījí	jīqì	xiǎoqū
xīngqī	xiāngjiāo	xìngqù	jìxù

z、c、s是舌尖前音。发z、c时，舌尖前部与上齿背接触，然后马上打开形成缝隙，z没有强烈的气流通过，而c有明显的气流通过。发s时，舌尖前与上齿背始终不接触，保留缝隙使气流流出。

z, *c* and *s* are dentals. When pronouncing *z* and *c*, the front part of the tongue tip touches the inner surface of the upper teeth and then immediately parts with it, forming a gap in between. *z* is pronounced with no strong airflow, while *c* comes with an obvious airflow. When pronouncing *s*, the front part of the tongue tip stays away from the inner surface of the upper teeth all along, leaving a gap for the airflow to get through.

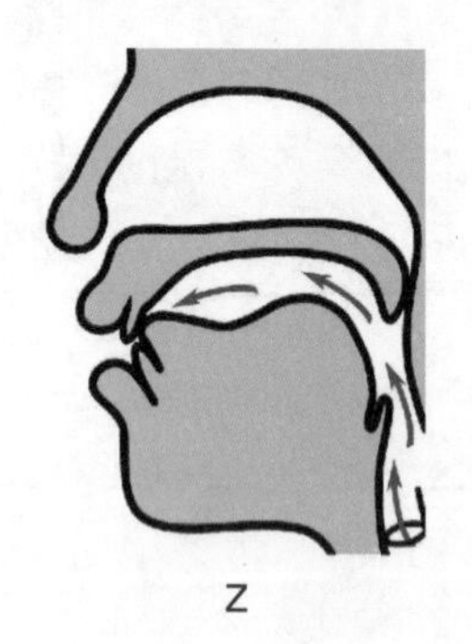

z

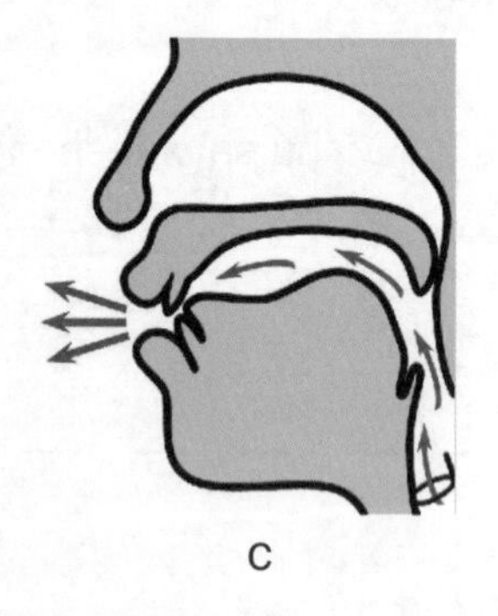

c

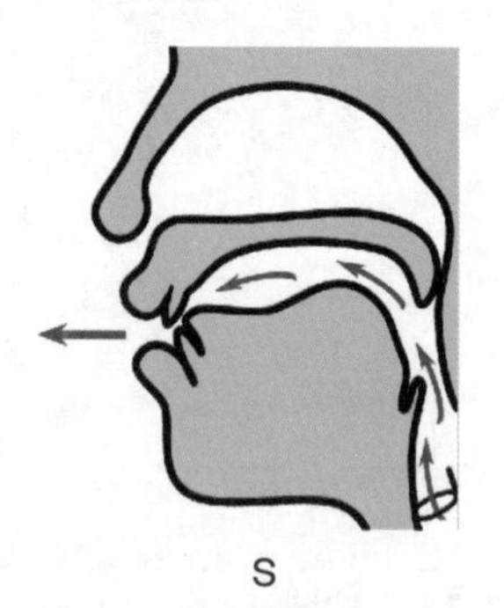

s

听录音并跟读，注意声母发音的区别 03-5

Listen to the recording and read after it. Pay attention to the differences between the initials.

xǐ zǎo	dǎsǎo	sān cì	zìjǐ
zuótiān	zǎoshang	cāochǎng	Hànzì

2 发音辨析：韵母i、u、ü Differentiation: pronunciation of the finals i, u, ü

i 和 ü 是发音位置相同、嘴唇形状不同的两个韵母，发 i 时嘴唇的形状是平的，而发 ü 时一定要圆唇。练习时可以先发好 i，保持发音部位不动，然后把嘴唇圆起来就可以发出 ü。

The finals *i* and *ü* share the same position of articulation, but are pronounced with the lips in different shapes. When pronouncing *i*, the lips are relaxed; when pronouncing *ü*, the lips must be rounded. To practice the two sounds, you can say *i* first, then keep your tongue where it is and round your lips to pronounce *ü*.

u 和 ü 都是圆唇音，但是发音时 ü 的舌位在前，舌尖抵住下齿背，而 u 的舌位在后，舌尖不能和下齿背接触，舌头要尽力往后收才能发对。

Both *u* and *ü* are pronounced with rounded lips. When saying *ü*, the tongue is in a front position, with the tip pressing the inner surface of the lower teeth; when saying *u*, the tongue is in a back position, with the tip staying away from the inner surface of the lower teeth, and the tongue should be held backwards to pronounce the sound right.

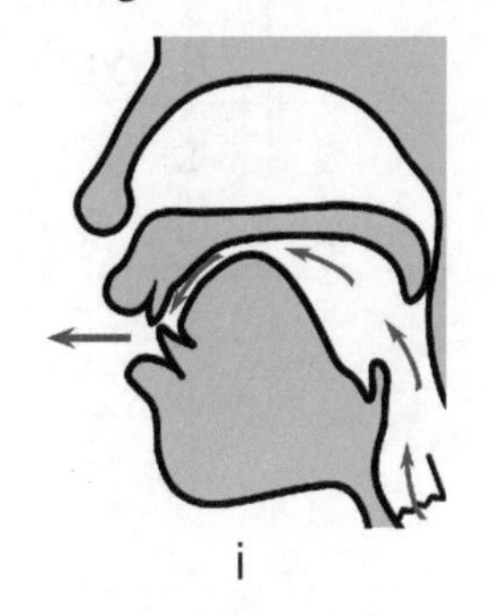
i

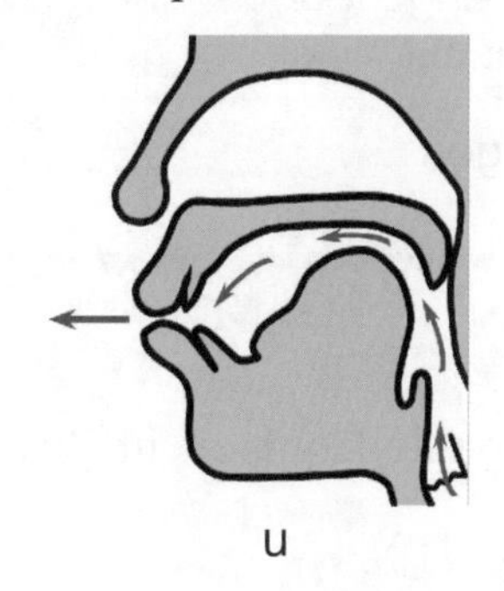
u

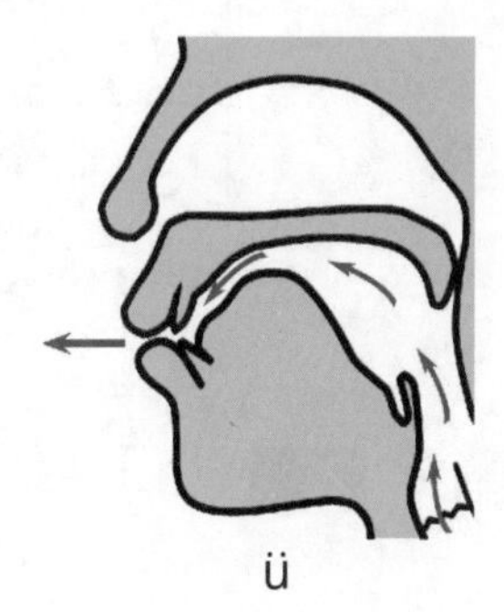
ü

3 "不"的变调 Tone Sandhi of "不 (bù)" 03-6

（1）"不"在第一、二、三声音节前不变调

When "不" is followed by a syllable in the first, second or third tone, its tone doesn't change.

bù chī	bù xíng	bù hǎo	bù hē	bù néng	bù xiǎng
to not eat	not OK	not good	to not drink	can't	don't want

（2）"不"在第四声音节前变成第二声

When "不" is followed by a syllable in the fourth tone, it changes into the second tone.

bú huì	bú shì	bú kàn
to be unable to	to be not	to not look

4 拼音规则（2）：单韵母 ü 和 ü 开头的韵母跟 j、q、x 相拼的规则

Rules of *Pinyin* (2): ü or finals led by ü with j, q, x

ü 和 ü 开头的韵母跟声母 j、q、x 相拼的时候，ü 上两点要省略，如写成 ju、qu、xu；但是跟声母 l、n 相拼的时候，仍然要写成 lü、nü。

When *ü* or a final beginning with *ü* follows *j*, *q* or *x*, the two dots on the top of *ü* should be removed, for example, *ju*, *qu*, *xu*. However, if the initial is *l* or *n*, the form is *lü* and *nü* respectively.

听录音并跟读，注意 ü 的拼写与实际发音 03-7

Listen to the recording and read after it. Pay attention to the form and pronunciation of *ü*.

ü	üe	üan	ün
ju	jue	juan	jun
qu	que	quan	qun
xu	xue	xuan	xun

汉字 Characters

1 汉字的笔画（3）：㇆、㇃

Strokes of Chinese Characters (3): ㇆, ㇃

笔画名称 Stroke	运笔方向 Direction	例字 Example Characters
㇆ 横折钩 héngzhégōu horizontal-turning-hook		门 mén door 月 yuè moon
㇃ 卧钩 wògōu lying hook		心 xīn heart 您 nín (*polite*) you

2 认识独体字 Single-Component Characters

（1）“月”，表示月亮。

“月” refers to the moon.

yuè

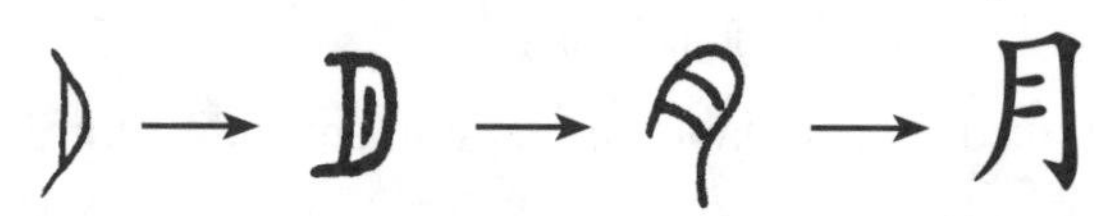

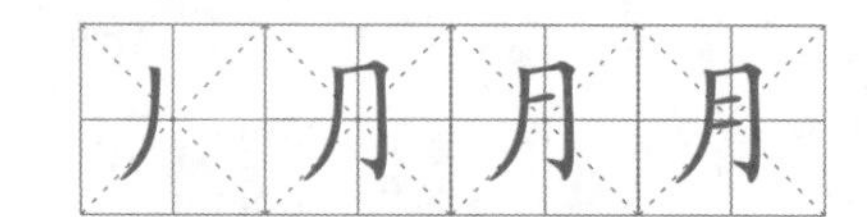

（2）“心”，表示心脏。

“心” refers to the heart.

xīn

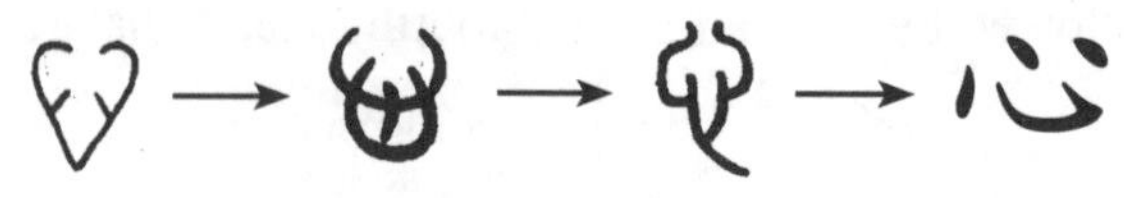

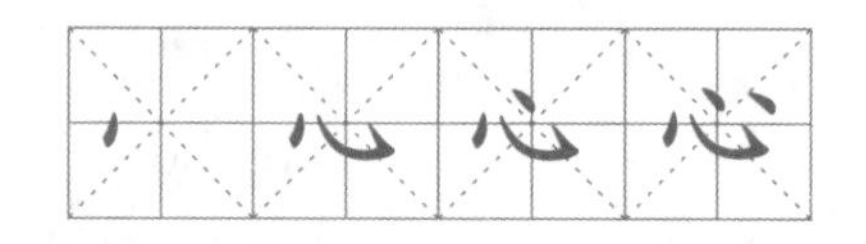

（3）“中”，本义是飘扬的旗子，现在表示方位，意思是“中间”。

The basic meaning of “中” is “flying flag”. It is now a word of locality, meaning “middle”.

zhōng

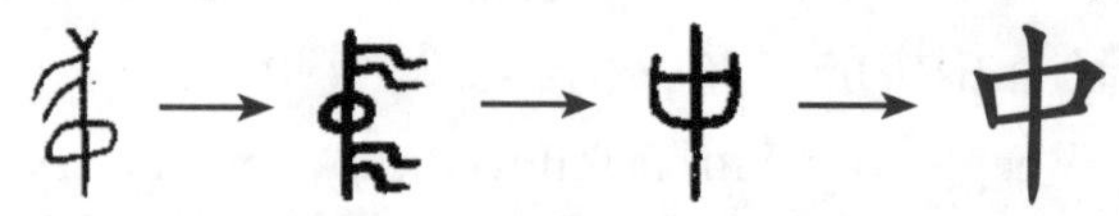

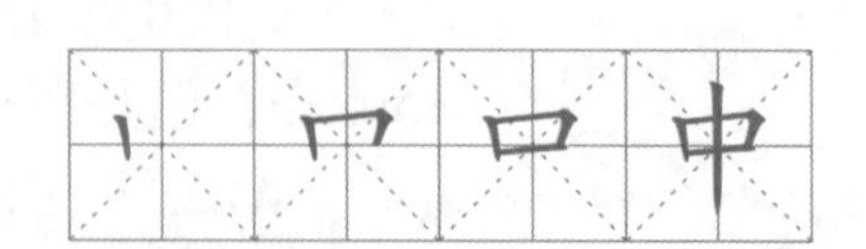

（4）“人”，表示直立的人。

“人” originally looked like a person standing straight.

rén

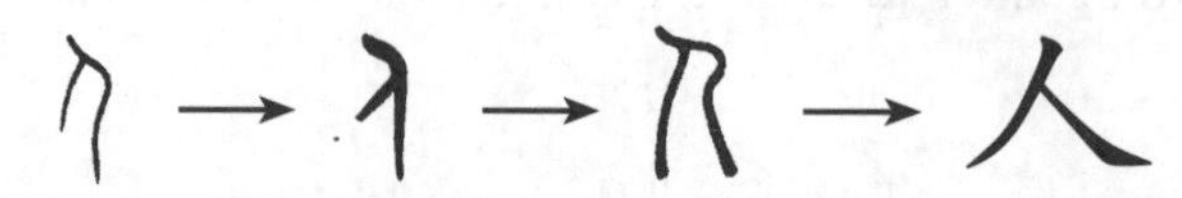

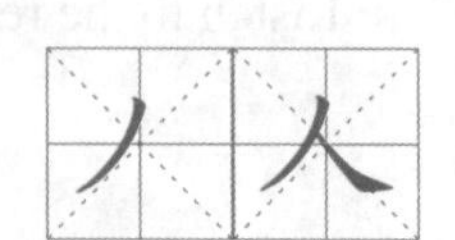

3 汉字的笔顺（1）：先横后竖，先撇后捺

Stroke Order (1): horizontal preceding vertical and left-falling preceding right-falling

笔顺 Rule	例字 Example Characters	书写顺序 Stroke Order
先横后竖 Horizontal preceding vertical	十 shí ten 工 gōng work, labor	一 十 一 丅 工
先撇后捺 Left-falling preceding right-falling	八 bā eight 人 rén human	丿 八 丿 人

运用 Application

1 双人活动 Pair Work

两人一组，进行自我介绍。

Work in pairs and introduce yourselves.

Wǒ jiào Lǐ Yuè, wǒ shì Zhōngguó rén, wǒ shì lǎoshī.

例如：A: 我 叫 李 月，我 是 中国 人，我 是 老师。

Wǒ jiào Dàwèi, wǒ shì Měiguó rén, wǒ shì xuésheng.

B: 我 叫 大卫（David），我 是 美国 人，我 是 学生。

2 小组活动 Group Work

3~4人一组，用汉语互相询问名字和国籍，每组请一位同学报告情况。

Work in groups of 3-4 and ask about each other's names and nationalities. Each group chooses one member to make a report.

	姓名 Name	国籍 Nationality
1	李月 Lǐ Yuè	中国 Zhōngguó

4 Tā shì wǒ de Hànyǔ lǎoshī 她是我的汉语老师 She is my Chinese teacher

热身 Warm-up

给下面的词语选择对应的图片
Match the pictures with the words/phrases.

A

B

C

D

E

F

① tā 他________ ② tā 她________ ③ tóngxué 同学________

④ péngyou 朋友________ ⑤ Hànyǔ lǎoshī 汉语老师________ ⑥ Zhōngguó péngyou 中国　朋友________

课文 Text

1 在教室 In the classroom 04-1

Tā shì shéi?
A: 她是谁？

Tā shì wǒ de Hànyǔ lǎoshī, tā jiào Lǐ Yuè.
B: 她是我的汉语老师，她叫李月。

English Version

A: Who is she?

B: She is my Chinese teacher. Her name is Li Yue.

New Words

1. 她	tā	pron.	she, her
2. 谁	shéi	pron.	who, whom
3. 的	de	part.	*used after an attribute*
4. 汉语	Hànyǔ	n.	Chinese (language)

2 在图书馆 In the library 04-2

Nǐ shì nǎ guó rén?
A: 你是哪国人?
Wǒ shì Měiguó rén. Nǐ ne?
B: 我是美国人。你呢?
Wǒ shì Zhōngguó rén.
A: 我是中国人。

English Version

A: Which country are you from?
B: The United States. What about you?
A: I'm Chinese.

New Words

5. 哪 nǎ pron. which
6. 国 guó n. country, nation
7. 呢 ne part. *used at the end of a question*

3 看照片 Looking at the photo 04-3

Tā shì shéi?
A: 他是谁?
Tā shì wǒ tóngxué.
B: 他是我同学。
Tā ne? Tā shì nǐ tóngxué ma?
A: 她呢? 她是你同学吗?
Tā bú shì wǒ tóngxué, tā shì wǒ péngyou.
B: 她不是我同学，她是我朋友。

English Version

A: Who is he?
B: He is my classmate.
A: What about her? Is she your classmate?
B: No, she isn't. She is my friend.

New Words

8. 他 tā pron. he, him
9. 同学 tóngxué n. classmate
10. 朋友 péngyou n. friend

注释 Notes

1 疑问代词“谁”、“哪” The Interrogative Pronouns “谁” and “哪”

疑问代词“谁”在疑问句中用来询问人。例如：

The interrogative pronoun “谁” is used to ask about the name or identity of a person. For example:

Subject	Verb	Object
谁	是	李月?
她	是	谁?
他	是	谁?

疑问代词“哪”用在疑问句中的结构形式为：哪+量词/名词+名词。例如：

When the interrogative pronoun “哪” is used in a question, the structure is “哪 + measure word/noun + noun”. For example:

（1）哪本（běn，*a measure word for books*）书（shū，book）？

（2）哪个（gè，*a general measure word*）人？

（3）你是哪国人？

2 结构助词“的” The Structural Particle “的”

名词/代词+的+名词 表达一种所属关系。当“的”后的名词是亲属称谓或者指人的名词时，“的”可以省略。例如：

The structure “noun/pronoun + 的 + noun” indicates possession. When the noun following “的” is a term of kinship or indicates a person, “的” can be omitted. For example:

（1）李月是我的老师。

（2）这（zhè，this）是我的书（shū，book）。

（3）她不是我同学，她是我朋友。

3 疑问助词“呢”（1） The Interrogative Particle “呢” (1)

疑问助词“呢”用在名词或代词后构成疑问句，用于询问上文提到的情况。常用的句式是：A……。B呢？ 例如：

The interrogative particle “呢” is used after a noun or pronoun, forming a question about the situation mentioned previously. The commonly used sentence pattern is “A……。B呢？” (A…. What about B?). For example:

（1）我不是老师，我是学生。你呢？

（2）她叫李月。他呢？

（3）我是美国人。你呢？

练习 Exercises

1 分角色朗读课文 Role-play the dialogues.

2 根据实际情况回答问题 Answer the questions according to the actual situations.

1. 你是哪国人？Nǐ shì nǎ guó rén?
2. 你叫什么名字？Nǐ jiào shénme míngzi?
3. 你的汉语老师是哪国人？Nǐ de Hànyǔ lǎoshī shì nǎ guó rén?
4. 你的汉语老师叫什么名字？Nǐ de Hànyǔ lǎoshī jiào shénme míngzi?
5. 你的中国朋友是谁？Nǐ de Zhōngguó péngyou shì shéi?

3 用本课新学的语言点和词语描述图片

Describe the pictures using the newly-learned language points and words.

Tā shì Qiáobùsī, tā shì ______ rén.
他是乔布斯(Steve Jobs)，他是______人。

Tā shì Lǐ Nà, tā shì ______ rén.
她是李娜(Li Na)，她是______人。

Tā jiào Mǎlì, tā bú shì wǒ ______, tā shì wǒ ______.
她叫玛丽(Mary)，她不是我______，她是我______。

Tā jiào Dàwèi, tā shì wǒmen de ______.
他叫大卫(David)，他是我们的______。

拼音 Pinyin

1 发音辨析：声母zh、ch、sh、r

Differentiation: pronunciation of the initials zh, ch, sh, r

zh、ch、sh、r是一组翘舌音，是由翘起的舌尖和硬腭前部配合而发音的。发zh、ch时，舌尖要先和硬腭接触，然后打开一条缝隙让气流通过，发zh时没有强烈的气流呼出，而发ch时呼出的气流很强。发sh时，舌尖不要与硬腭接触，要始终保持一条缝隙。与sh不同，在发r时声带要振动。

zh, *ch*, *sh* and *r* are a series of cacuminals, which are pronounced with the tongue tip turned-up and coordinating with the front part of the hard palate. When saying *zh* and *ch*, the tongue tip first touches the hard palate and then opens a gap to let the air flow. *ch* comes with a much stronger airflow, but *zh* doesn't. When saying *sh*, the tongue tip doesn't touch the hard palate, leaving a gap all along. Different from *sh*, *r* is pronounced with the vocal cords vibrating.

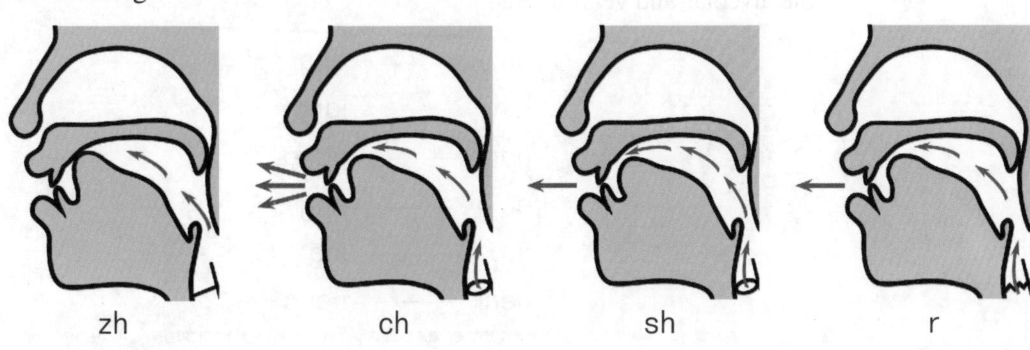

听录音并跟读，注意声母发音的区别 04-4

Listen to the recording and read after it. Pay attention to the differences between the initials.

zhīshi	chúshī	shēngrì	shàng chē
rènshi	chángshí	shìshí	chāorén
ránshāo	rènao	chū chāi	Chángchéng
shǒushù	shāngchǎng	chāoshì	chōng zhí

2 发音辨析：前鼻音韵母 n 和后鼻音韵母 ng

Differentiation: pronunciation of the alveolar nasal n and the velar nasal ng

发前鼻音 n [n] 时舌尖要抵住上齿龈，而发后鼻音 ng [ŋ] 时，舌头的后部要拱起，舌根向后收缩，抵住软腭；发 n[n]时上下齿相对，开口较小，而发 ng [ŋ] 时开口度较大。

When saying the alveolar nasal *n* [n], the tongue tip should press the upper alveolar ridge; when saying the velar nasal *ng* [ŋ], the back part of the tongue forms an arch and the root of the tongue moves back and presses the soft palate. Compared with *n* [n], which is pronounced with the upper and lower teeth close to each other, *ng* [ŋ] is pronounced with the mouth more wide-open.

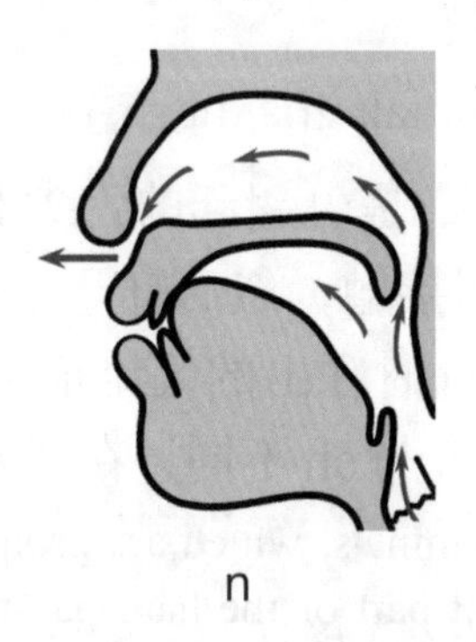
n

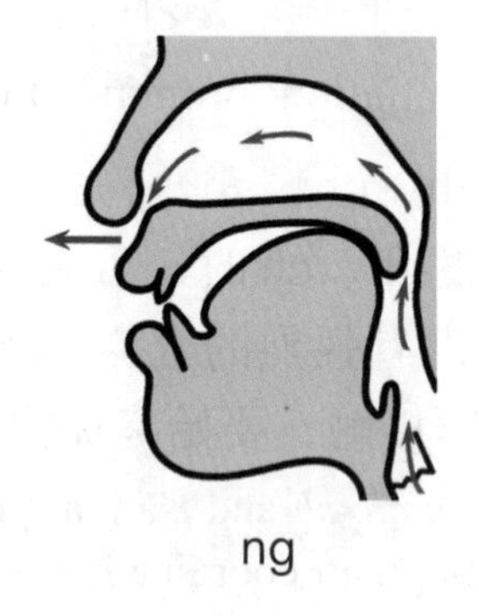
ng

听录音并跟读，注意前后鼻音韵母发音的区别 04-5

Listen to the recording and read after it. Pay attention to the differences between the alveolar and velar nasals.

an —— ang
ian —— iang
uan —— uang
en —— eng
in —— ing
uen —— ueng

3 "一"的变调 Tone Sandhi of "一 (yī)" 04-6

（1）"一"在第一、二、三声音节前变成第四声

When "一" is followed by a syllable in the first, second or third tone, it changes into the fourth tone.

yì zhāng	yì tiáo	yì zhǒng
one sheet/piece	one (long) piece	one type

（2）"一"在第四声音节前变成第二声

When "一" is followed by a syllable in the fourth, it changes into the second tone.

yídìng	yí kuài
sure, certainly	one piece

（3）"一"单用或表示数字时不变调

When "一" is used alone or in a number, its tone doesn't change.

dì yī	yī èr sān	xīngqī yī	shíyī	bǎifēnzhī yī
first	one, two, three	Monday	eleven	one percent

4 拼音规则（3）：y、w的用法

Rules of *Pinyin* (3): use of y and w

以i、u、ü开头的韵母如果前面没有声母，在拼写时需要使用y或w，具体情况如下：

If a final beginning with *i*, *u* or *ü* has no initial before it, *y* or *w* is used in the written form. See the following table for details:

韵母 Final		写法 Written Form
Beginning with *i*	i、in、ing	yi、yin、ying
	ia、ie、iao、ian、iang、iong	ya、ye、yao、yan、yang、yong
	iu	you
Beginning with *u*	u	wu
	ua、uo、uai、uan、uang、ueng	wa、wo、wai、wan、wang、weng
	ui、un	wei、wen
Beginning with *ü*	ü、üe、üan、ün	yu、yue、yuan、yun

听录音并跟读，注意 y、w 的用法 04-7

Listen to the recording and read after it. Pay attention to the use of *y* and *w*.

yóu yǒng	yǒuyì	yīnyuè	yuányīn
qīngwā	yǐngxīng	yīngxióng	wēixiǎn
guó wài	yīntiān	yǔyán	wǎngwǎng
wǎnyàn	yéye	yíngyǎng	wǒmen

汉字 Characters

1 汉字的笔画（4）：乚、乙

Strokes of Chinese Characters (4): 乚，乙

笔画名称 Stroke	运笔方向 Direction	例字 Example Characters
乚 竖弯钩 shùwāngōu vertical curved hook		七 qī seven 儿 ér son
乙 横折弯钩 héngzhéwāngōu horizontal-turning curved hook		九 jiǔ nine 几 jǐ how many

2 认识独体字 Single-Component Characters

（1）"七"，表示数量"7"。

"七" means "seven".

qī

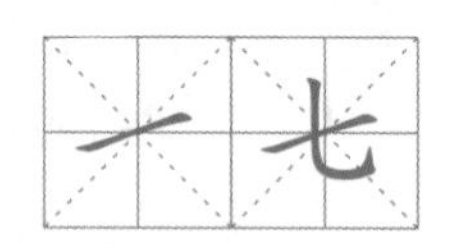

（2）"儿"，本义是小孩。现在多指儿子。

"儿" originally meant "kid", but now it usually means "son".

ér

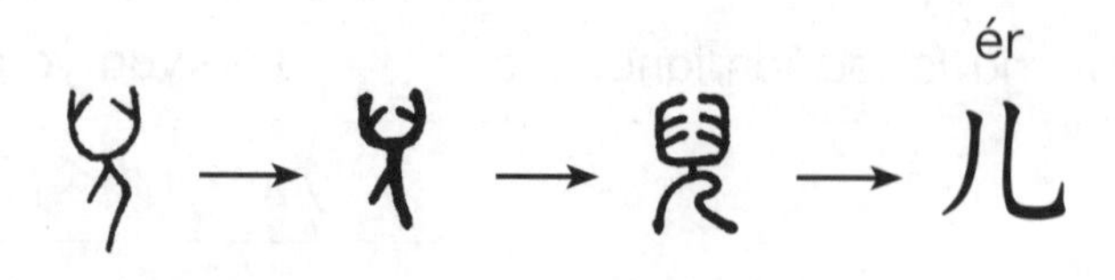

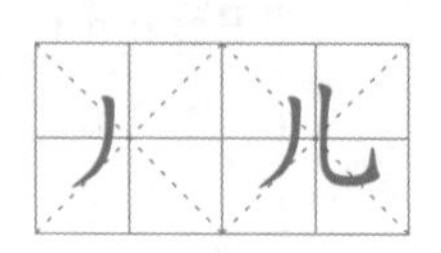

（3）"几"，本义是小矮桌。

"几" originally referred to a small and low table.

jǐ

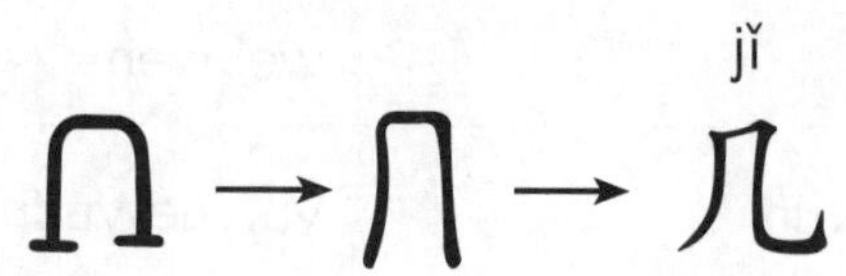

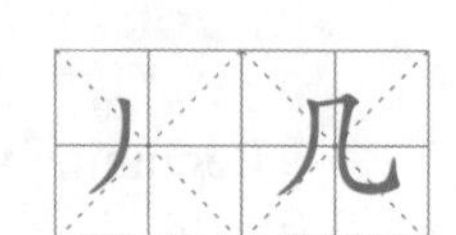

（4）“九”，表示数量“9”。

“九” means “nine”.

jiǔ

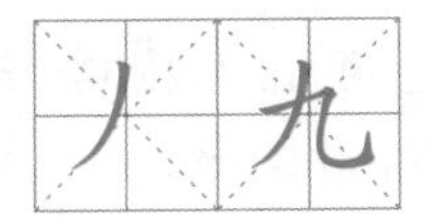

3 汉字的笔顺（2）：从上到下，从左到右

Stroke Order (2): top preceding bottom and left preceding right

笔顺 Rule	例字 Example Characters	书写顺序 Stroke Order
从上到下 Top preceding bottom	二 èr two 三 sān three	一 二 一 二 三
从左到右 Left preceding right	几 jǐ how many 八 bā eight	丿 几 丿 八

运用 Application

1 双人活动 Pair Work

两人一组，根据图片内容进行问答练习。

Work in pairs and ask and answer questions based on the pictures.

例如：A: Tā/Tā shì shéi? 他/她是谁？ B: Tā/Tā shì…… 他/她是……

A: Tā/Tā shì nǎ guó rén? 他/她是哪国人？ B: Tā/Tā shì…… 他/她是……

2 小组活动 Group Work

3~4人一组，每人准备一张自己和同学或者朋友的合影，向同组成员介绍照片上的人物。

Work in groups of 3-4. Prepare a photo of you and your classmates or friends and introduce the people in the photo to your group members.

例如：Tā/Tā shì wǒ tóngxué/péngyou, tā/tā jiào……, tā/tā shì……

他/她是我同学/朋友，他/她叫……，他/她是……

5 Tā nǚ'ér jīnnián èrshí suì
她女儿今年二十岁
Her daughter is 20 years old this year

热身 Warm-up

给下面的词语选择对应的图片
Match the pictures with the words/phrases.

liù kǒu rén	jiā	nǚ'ér
① 六口人＿＿＿＿	② 家＿＿＿＿	③ 女儿＿＿＿＿
xuésheng	qīshí suì	èrshí suì
④ 学生＿＿＿＿	⑤ 70 岁＿＿＿＿	⑥ 20 岁＿＿＿＿

课文 Text

1 在学校 In the school 05-1

Nǐ jiā yǒu jǐ kǒu rén?
A: 你家有几口人？

Wǒ jiā yǒu sān kǒu rén.
B: 我家有三口人。

English Version

A: How many people are there in your family?

B: There are three.

New Words

1. 家 jiā n. family
2. 有 yǒu v. to have, there be

*3. 口 kǒu m. *a measure word for members of families, etc.*

2 在办公室 In the office 05-2

Nǐ nǚ'ér jǐ suì le?
A: 你女儿几岁了？
Tā jīnnián sì suì le.
B: 她今年四岁了。

English Version

A: How old is your daughter?
B: She is four years old.

New Words

4. 女儿 nǚ'ér n. daughter
5. 几 jǐ pron. how many
6. 岁 suì m. year (of age)
7. 了 le part. *used at the end of or in the middle of a sentence to indicate a change or a new circumstance*
8. 今年 jīnnián n. this year

3 在办公室 In the office 05-3

Lǐ lǎoshī duō dà le?
A: 李老师多大了？
Tā jīnnián wǔshí suì le.
B: 她今年 50 岁了。
Tā nǚ'ér ne?
A: 她女儿呢？
Tā nǚ'ér jīnnián èrshí suì.
B: 她女儿今年 20 岁。

English Version

A: How old is Professor Li?
B: She is 50 years old.
A: What about her daughter?
B: Her daughter is 20.

New Words

9. 多 duō adv. *indicating degree or extent*
10. 大 dà adj. (of age) old

注释 Notes

1 疑问代词“几” The Interrogative Pronoun “几”

疑问代词“几”用来询问数量的多少，一般用于询问10以下的数字。例如：

The interrogative pronoun “几” is used to ask about a number, usually less than 10. For example:

（1）你有几个汉语老师？

（2）李老师家有几口人？

（3）你女儿几岁了？

2 百以内的数字 Numbers below 100

	1 yī	2 èr	3 sān	4 sì	5 wǔ	6 liù	7 qī	8 bā	9 jiǔ
10 shí									19 shíjiǔ
20 èrshí			23 èrshísān						
30 sānshí									
40 sìshí									
50 wǔshí						56 wǔshíliù			
60 liùshí									
70 qīshí									
80 bāshí								88 bāshíbā	
90 jiǔshí									99 jiǔshíjiǔ

3 “了”表变化 “了” Indicating a Change

“了”用于句末，表示变化或新情况的出现。例如：

“了” is used at the end of a sentence to indicate a change or the occurrence of a new situation. For example:

（1）李老师今年50岁了。

（2）我朋友的女儿今年四岁了。

（3）你女儿几岁了？

4 “多+大”表示疑问 The Interrogative Phrase “多+大”

“多+大”在句中表示疑问，用于询问年龄。例如：

“多+大” is used to ask about one’s age. For example:

（1）你多大了？

（2）你女儿今年多大了？

（3）李老师多大了？

练习 Exercises

1 分角色朗读课文 Role-play the dialogues.

2 根据实际情况回答问题 Answer the questions according to the actual situations.

① 你家有几口人？ Nǐ jiā yǒu jǐ kǒu rén?

② 你今年多大了？ Nǐ jīnnián duō dà le?

③ 你的汉语老师今年多大了？ Nǐ de Hànyǔ lǎoshī jīnnián duō dà le?

④ 你的中国朋友家有几口人？ Nǐ de Zhōngguó péngyou jiā yǒu jǐ kǒu rén?

⑤ 你的中国朋友今年多大了？ Nǐ de Zhōngguó péngyou jīnnián duō dà le?

3 用本课新学的语言点和词语描述图片

Describe the pictures using the newly-learned language points and words.

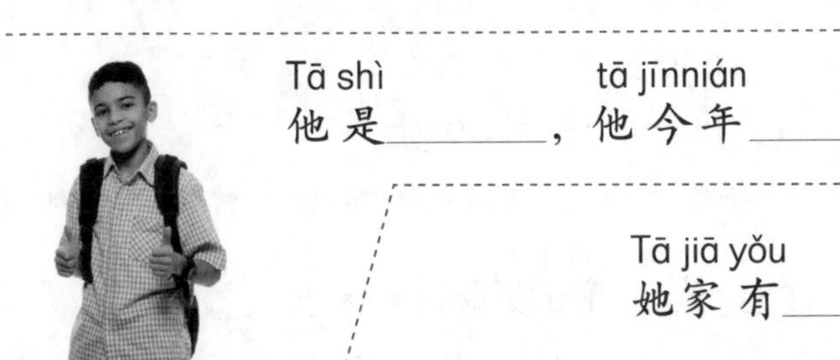

Tā shì ______, tā jīnnián ______ le.
他是______，他今年______了。

Tā jiā yǒu ______ rén.
她家有______人。

Tā shì wǒmen de Hànyǔ ______, tā jīnnián ______ le.
他是我们的汉语______，他今年______了。

Zhè shì Zhāng lǎoshī de ______, tā jīnnián ______ le.
这是张老师的______，她今年______了。

拼音 Pinyin

1 儿化的发音 The Retroflex Final 05-4

汉语中的“儿”可以和前面的音节结合成为一个音节，变成“儿化音”。汉字书写时表示为“汉字+儿”，拼音书写时在该汉字的拼音后加“r”。例如：

“儿 (ér) ” can be combined with a syllable before it, forming a retroflex syllable, which is written as “character + 儿” and spelt “syllable + r” in *pinyin*. For example:

xiǎoháir
小孩儿

xiǎo niǎor
小 鸟儿

fànguǎnr
饭馆儿

xiāngshuǐr
香水儿

2 发音辨析：以 i、u、ü 开头的韵母

Differentiation: pronunciation of finals beginning with i, u, ü

听录音并跟读，注意有 i、无 i 时发音的区别 05-5

Listen to the recording and read after it. Pay attention to the differences between the pronunciations of the finals with and without *i*.

a —— ia
e —— ie
ao —— iao
ou —— iou（iu）
an —— ian
ang —— iang
ong —— iong

听录音并跟读，注意有 u 、无 u 发音时的区别 05-6

Listen to the recording and read after it. Pay attention to the differences between the pronunciations of the finals with and without *u*.

a —— ua
ai —— uai
ei —— uei（ui）
an —— uan
en —— uen（un）
ang —— uang
eng —— ueng

听录音并跟读，注意有 ü 、无 ü 发音时的区别 05-7

Listen to the recording and read after it. Pay attention to the differences between the pronunciations of the finals with and without *ü*.

e —— üe

an —— üan

en —— ün

3 声母送气音和不送气音发音的区别

Difference between Aspirated and Unaspirated Initials

汉语声母的发音有送气和不送气的区别，b–p，d–t，g–k，j–q，z–c，zh–ch，以上各组声母中前一个是不送气音，后一个音是送气音。

There are aspirated and unaspirated initials in Chinese, such as *b-p*, *d-t*, *g-k*, *j-q*, *z-c* and *zh-ch*, among which the first one in each pair is unaspirated and the second one is aspirated.

听录音并跟读，注意送气音和不送气音发音的区别 05-8

Listen to the recording and read after it. Pay attention to the differences between the aspirated and unaspirated initials.

b — p　　d — t　　g — k　　j — q　　z — c　　zh — ch

听录音并跟读，注意声母发音的区别 05-9

Listen to the recording and read after it. Pay attention to the differences between the initials.

bàng — pàng　　dù — tù　　gǒu — kǒu

jī — qī　　zì — cì　　zhuō — chē

4 拼音规则（4）：隔音符号

Rules of *Pinyin* (4): syllable-dividing mark

a、o、e开头的音节连接在其他音节后面时，为了避免音节的界限发生混淆，用隔音符号（’）隔开，例如 pí’ǎo（皮袄）。

When a syllable beginning with *a*, *o* or *e* follows another syllable, the syllable-dividing mark (’) is used to separate the two syllables, for example, *pí’ǎo* (皮袄, fur-lined jacket).

听录音并跟读，注意有无隔音符号的不同 05-10

Listen to the recording and read after it. Pay attention to the differences between the words with and without the syllable-dividing mark.

piāo — pí'ǎo
to float – fur-lined jacket

xiān — Xī'ān
earlier, before – City of Xi'an

jiē — jī'è
to receive – hungry

jiāng — jī'áng
will, shall – excited and impassioned

fānàn — fān'àn
to launch an attack – to reverse a verdict

fǎngǎn — fāng'àn
to loathe – work plan

汉字 Characters

1 汉字的笔画（5）：㇇、㇛

Strokes of Chinese Characters (5): ㇇, ㇛

笔画名称 Stroke	运笔方向 Direction	例字 Example Characters
㇇ 横撇 héngpiě horizontal to left-falling	㇇	水 shuǐ water 又 yòu again
㇛ 撇点 piědiǎn left-falling to dot	㇛	女 nǚ female, woman 好 hǎo good, fine

2 认识独体字 Single-Component Characters

（1）“水”，字形像山涧，表示水流的形状。

“水” originally looked like a mountain stream, representing the shape of the flowing water.

shuǐ

→ → → 水

（2）“女”，字形像一个跪在地上的女人，意思是“女人”。

“女” originally looked like a woman kneeling down on the ground, meaning “woman”.

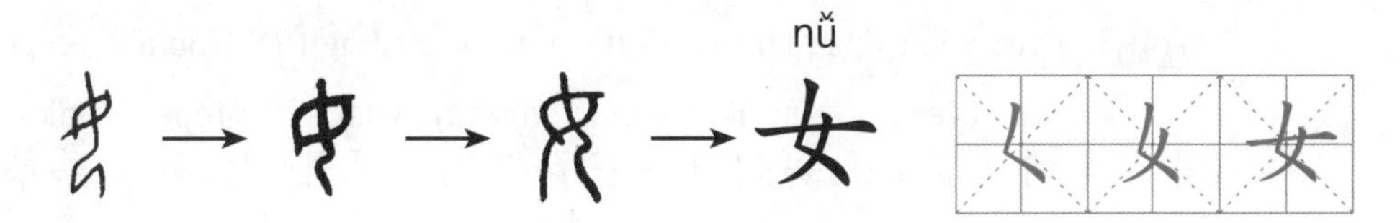

（3）“了”，字形像 ɓ（头朝下、未出生的胎儿）的倒写，头朝上，表示已经出生的婴儿。现在成为虚词。

“了” originally looked like a reversed ɓ (an unborn foetus in a head-down position). With the head on top, it referred to a baby already born. Now it is a function word.

（4）“大”，本义是张开双手双腿顶天立地的人，现在意思与“小”相对。

“大” originally referred to a person in a standing position, with his arms and legs stretching out. Now it means “big”, opposite to “小 (small)”.

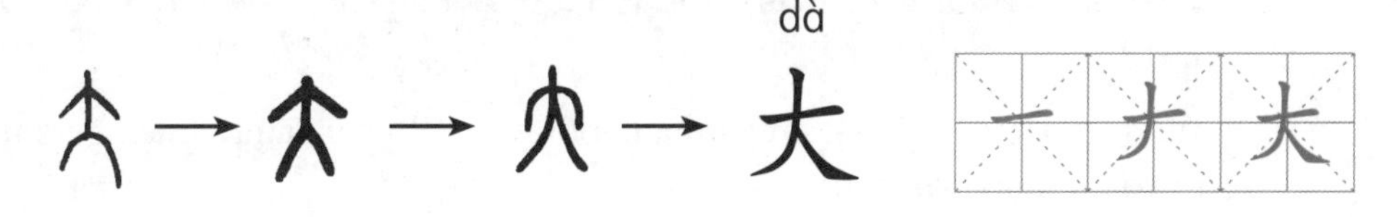

3 汉字的笔顺（3）：先外后内，先中间后两边

Stroke Order (3): outside preceding inside and middle preceding sides

笔顺 Rule	例字 Example Characters	书写顺序 Stroke Order
先外后内 Outside preceding inside	四 sì four 国 guó country	丨 冂 𠃜 四 四 丨 冂 冂 冃 円 囯 国 国
先中间后两边 Middle preceding sides	小 xiǎo small 水 shuǐ water	亅 小 小 亅 才 水 水

运用 Application

1 双人活动 Pair Work

两人一组，根据实际情况进行问答练习。

Work in pairs and ask and answer questions according to the actual situations.

yéye nǎinai bàba māma gēge jiějie dìdi mèimei
补充生词：爷爷、奶奶、爸爸、妈妈、哥哥、姐姐、弟弟、妹妹

Supplementary words: (paternal) grandpa, (paternal) grandma, father, mother, elder brother, elder sister, younger brother, younger sister

Nǐ jiā yǒu jǐ kǒu rén?
例如：A: 你家有几口人？

Wǒ jiā yǒu……
B: 我家有……

Nǐ/Nǐ bàba/Nǐ māma……jīnnián duō dà le?
A: 你/你爸爸/你妈妈……今年多大了？

Wǒ/Wǒ bàba/Wǒ māma……jīnnián……
B: 我/我爸爸/我妈妈……今年……

2 小组活动 Group Work

3~4人一组，每人准备一张自己全家的合影，向同组成员介绍家庭成员的情况。

Work in groups of 3-4. Prepare a photo with all your family members in it. Introduce them to your group members.

Wǒ jiā yǒu……rén.
例如：我家有……人。

Zhè shì wǒ……, zhè shì wǒ……, zhè shì wǒ……
这是我……，这是我……，这是我……

……jiào……, tā / tā shì……, tā / tā jīnnián ……le.
……叫……，他/她是……，他/她今年……了。

文化 CULTURE

中国人对年龄的询问方法 Ways of Asking a Chinese Person's Age

在中国传统文化中，年龄并不被认为是一种个人隐私，在社交中是人们常常涉及的问题。但询问不同的人的年龄，表达方式也不尽相同。对于10岁以下的孩子，一般用"你今年几岁了？"来提问；对青年人或者和自己年纪相仿的人，一般可以问"你今年多大了？"；出于对长者的尊敬，询问年长的人的年龄则一定要用"您今年多大年纪了？"

In traditional Chinese culture, age isn't considered privacy. It is a topic often brought up in social occasions. Nevertheless, different ways are employed to ask about the age of different people. For kids younger than 10, people ask "你今年几岁了？(How old are you?)"; for a young person or someone of one's own age, one may ask "你今年多大了？(How old are you?)"; for an elder person, however, one should use "您今年多大年纪了？(What's your age?)" to show respect.

6 Wǒ huì shuō Hànyǔ 我会说汉语 I can speak Chinese

热身 Warm-up

给下面的词语选择对应的图片

Match the pictures with the words/phrases.

A 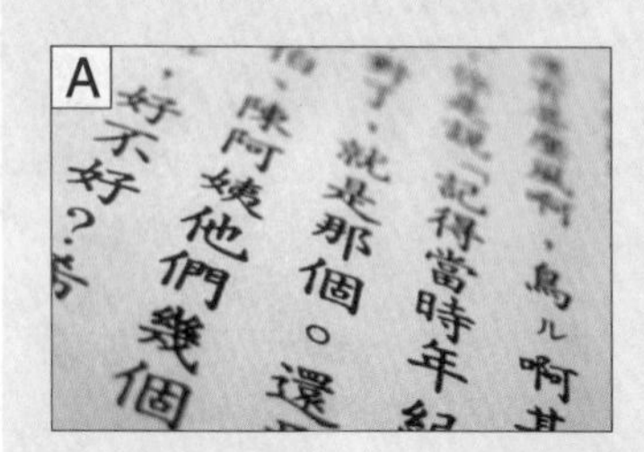

B 

C 

D 

E 

F 

māma ① 妈妈 ________	Hànzì ② 汉字 ________	Zhōngguó cài ③ 中国 菜 ________
shuō Hànyǔ ④ 说 汉语 ________	xiě Hànzì ⑤ 写汉字 ________	zuò Zhōngguó cài ⑥ 做 中国 菜 ________

课文 Text

1 在学校 In the school 06-1

Nǐ huì shuō Hànyǔ ma?
A: 你会 说 汉语 吗?

Wǒ huì shuō Hànyǔ.
B: 我 会 说 汉语。

Nǐ māma huì shuō Hànyǔ ma?
A: 你妈妈 会 说 汉语 吗?

Tā bú huì shuō.
B: 她不会 说。

English Version

A: Can you speak Chinese?

B: Yes, I can.

A: Can your mother speak Chinese?

B: No, she can't.

New Words

1. 会 huì mod. can, to be able to
2. 说 shuō v. to speak, to say
3. 妈妈 māma n. mother

2 在厨房 In the kitchen 06-2

Zhōngguó cài hǎo chī ma?
A: 中国 菜好吃吗？
Zhōngguó cài hěn hǎochī.
B: 中国 菜很好吃。
Nǐ huì zuò Zhōngguó cài ma?
A: 你会做 中国 菜吗？
Wǒ bú huì zuò.
B: 我不会做。

English Version

A: Is Chinese food delicious?
B: Yes, quite delicious.
A: Can you cook Chinese food?
B: No, I can't.

New Words

4. 菜 cài n. dish, cuisine
5. 很 hěn adv. very, quite
*6. 好吃 hǎochī adj. delicious, tasty
7. 做 zuò v. to make, to produce

3 在图书馆 In the library 06-3

Nǐ huì xiě Hànzì ma?
A: 你会写汉字吗？
Wǒ huì xiě.
B: 我会写。
Zhège zì zěnme xiě?
A: 这个字怎么写？
Duìbuqǐ, zhège zì wǒ huì dú, bú huì xiě.
B: 对不起，这个字我会读，不会写。

English Version

A: Can you write Chinese characters?
B: Yes, I can.
A: How do you write this character?
B: Sorry. I can read it, but I don't know how to write it.

New Words

8. 写 xiě v. to write
9. 汉字 Hànzì n. Chinese character
10. 字 zì n. character, word
11. 怎么 zěnme pron. (*indicating nature, condition or manner, etc.*) how
12. 读 dú v. to read

注释 Notes

1 能愿动词“会”（1） The Modal Verb “会” (1)

能愿动词“会”用在动词前表示通过学习而获得某种能力，它的否定式是“不会”。例如：

The modal verb “会” is used before a verb, indicating acquiring an ability through learning. Its negative form is “不会”. For example:

Subject	（不）会	Verb
我	会	写汉字。
我	不会	做中国菜。
你妈妈	会	说汉语吗？

2 形容词谓语句 Sentences with an Adjectival Predicate

形容词可以用在 主语+程度副词+形容词 这个结构中，描述人或事物的性质或状态，程度副词经常用“很”。否定形式为 主语+不+形容词 。例如：

Used in the structure “subject + adverb of degree + adjective”, the adjective describes the nature or state of somebody or something, usually following the adverb of degree “很”. The negative form is “subject + 不 + adjective”. For example:

Subject	Adverb of Degree/不	Adjective
我	很	好。
我妈妈的汉语	不	好。
中国菜	很	好吃。

3 疑问代词“怎么”（1） The Interrogative Pronoun “怎么” (1)

疑问代词“怎么”用在动词前，询问动作的方式。例如：

The interrogative pronoun “怎么” is used before a verb to ask about the manner of an action. For example:

（1）这个汉字怎么读？

（2）你的汉语名字怎么写？

（3）这个字怎么写？

练习 Exercises

1 分角色朗读课文 Role-play the dialogues.

2 根据实际情况回答问题 Answer the questions according to the actual situations.

1. 你会说汉语吗？Nǐ huì shuō Hànyǔ ma?
2. 你会写汉字吗？Nǐ huì xiě Hànzì ma?
3. 你会做中国菜吗？Nǐ huì zuò Zhōngguó cài ma?
4. 你有汉语名字吗？Nǐ yǒu Hànyǔ míngzi ma?
5. 你会写你的汉语名字吗？Nǐ huì xiě nǐ de Hànyǔ míngzi ma?

3 用本课新学的语言点和词语描述图片

Describe the pictures using the newly-learned language points and words.

Wǒmen dōu huì
我们 都 会________。

Zhōngguó cài hěn
中国 菜 很________。

Tā huì zuò
他 会 做________。

Zhège Hànzì wǒ huì
这个 汉字 我 会________，
bú huì
不 会________。

拼音 Pinyin

双音节词语的声调搭配（1）：一声和各声调的搭配

Tone Collocation in Disyllabic Words (1): 1st tone + 1st/2nd/3rd/4th tone

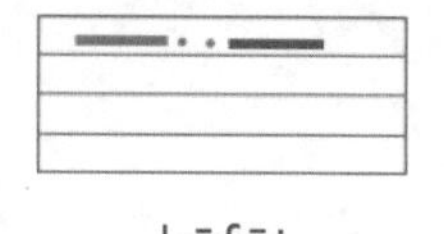
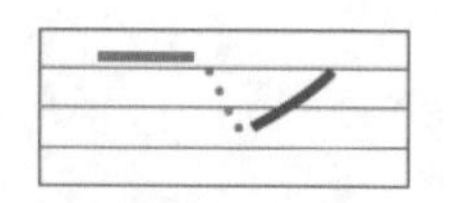
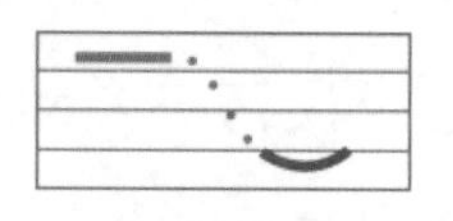
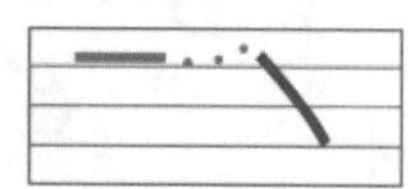

kāfēi 咖啡	gōngyuán 公园	jīchǎng 机场	chēzhàn 车站

*注意：在音节组合中，第三声的发音和单音节第三声的发音（214）不同，是一个近似于211的低降调，音节的后半部分不再升高。

Note: The third tone in collocation is pronounced differently from the third tone used alone(214). It's a falling tone with a pitch approximate to 211, which means its latter half won't rise as it normally does when used alone.

听录音并跟读，注意声调的搭配 06-4

Listen to the recording and read after it. Pay attention to the collocation of tones.

jīntiān	jīnnián	jīngcǎi	chēpiào
gōngsī	gāngcái	cāochǎng	jīdàn
guā fēng	huānyíng	jīnglǐ	jīhuì
guānxīn	guānyú	kāishǐ	gāoxìng

汉字 Characters

1 汉字的笔画（6）：㇜、㇂、㇀

Strokes of Chinese Characters (6): ㇜, ㇂, ㇀

笔画名称 Stroke	运笔方向 Direction	例字 Example Characters
㇜ 撇折 piězhé left-falling to turning		么 me *a suffix* 东 dōng east
㇂ 斜钩 xiégōu slanting hook		我 wǒ I, me 钱 qián money
㇀ 提 tí rising		我 wǒ I, me 打 dǎ to beat, to hit

2 认识独体字 Single-Component Characters

（1）“东”，太阳升起的一边，意思与“西”相对。

“东 (east)” is where the sun rises. It’s opposite to “西 (west)” in meaning.

dōng

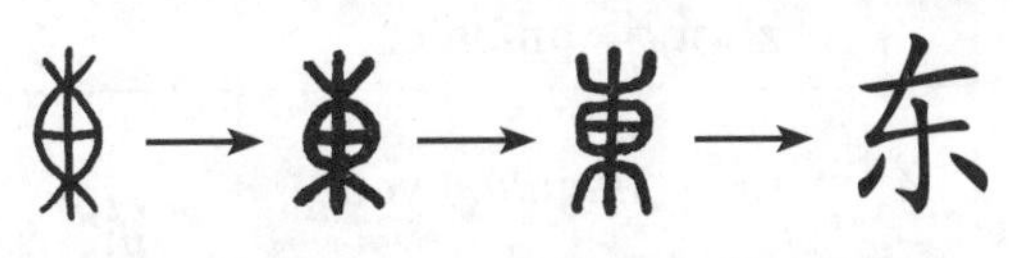

（2）“我”，字形像一种有许多利齿的武器，现在演变成代词。

The character “我” originally looked like a weapon with sharp, pointed edges. Now it is a personal pronoun.

wǒ

我

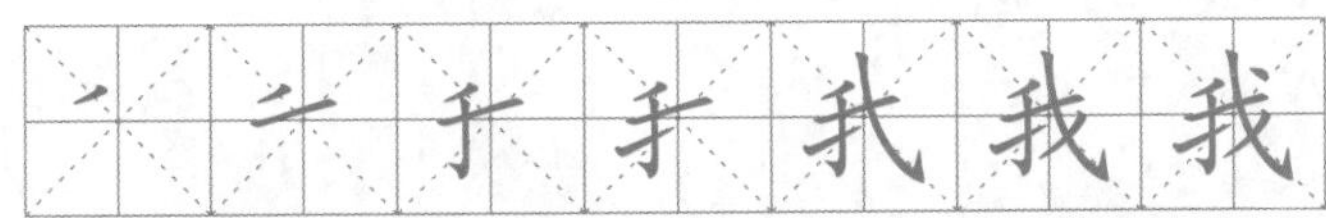

（3）“西”，字形像鸟巢的形状，现在表示方位，与“东”相对。

“西” was originally shaped like a bird’s nest. Now it means “west”, opposite to “东 (east)”.

xī

西

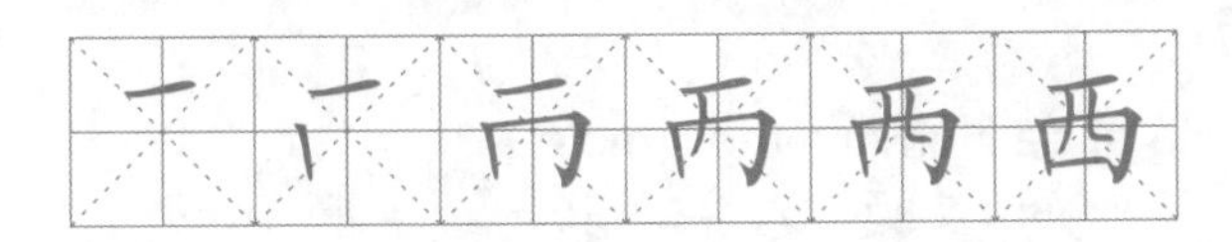

3 汉字结构（1）：独体结构与合体结构

Structure of Chinese Characters (1): single-component and compound

汉字的结构基本有两种，只由一个部分构成的汉字结构叫作“独体结构”，比如，“人”；由两个或者两个以上部分构成的汉字结构叫作“合体结构”，比如“你”。

Basically Chinese characters fall into two types of structures: the single-component structure and the compound structure. The former has only one component, for example, “人”; while the latter is made up of two or more components, for example, “你”.

结构 Structure	例字 Example Characters	图解 Illustrations
独体结构 single	人 rén human 我 wǒ I, me 中 zhōng middle	人 我 中
合体结构 compound	你 nǐ (*singular*) you 做 zuò to do	你 做

运用 Application

1 双人活动 Pair Work

两人一组，根据实际情况进行问答练习。

Work in pairs and ask and answer questions according to the actual situations.

例如：A: Nǐ huì shuō Hànyǔ ma?
你 会 说 汉语 吗？

B: Wǒ
我……

A: Nǐ huì xiě Hànzì ma?
你 会 写 汉字 吗？

B: Wǒ
我……

A: Nǐ de Hànyǔ míngzi jiào shénme?
你的 汉语 名字 叫 什么？

B: Wǒ de
我 的……

A: Nǐ huì xiě nǐ de Hànyǔ míngzi ma?
你 会 写你的 汉语 名字 吗？

B: ……

2 小组活动 Group Work

3~4人一组，互相询问所掌握的言语技能并记录，每组请一位同学报告情况。

Work in groups of 3-4. Ask about each other's language skills and take notes. Each group chooses one member to make a report.

补充生词：Yīngyǔ、Fǎyǔ、Rìyǔ
英语、法语、日语

Supplementary words: English, French, Japanese

	姓名 Name	英语 English	法语 French	汉语 Chinese	日语 Japanese	
1	大卫 Dàwèi	✓	✓	×	×	

7 Jīntiān jǐ hào 今天几号 What's the date today

热身 Warm-up

给下面的词语选择对应的图片
Match the pictures with the words/phrases.

A 

B 

C 

D 

E 

F 

① shū 书________
② Zhōngguó cài 中国菜________
③ xuéxiào 学校________
④ èrshíwǔ hào 25号________
⑤ yuè 月________
⑥ kàn shū 看书________

课文 Text

1 在银行 In a bank 07-1

Qǐngwèn, jīntiān jǐ hào?
A: 请问，今天几号？

Jīntiān jiǔ yuè yī hào.
B: 今天9月1号。

Jīntiān xīngqī jǐ?
A: 今天星期几？

Xīngqī sān.
B: 星期三。

English Version

A: Excuse me, what's the date today?
B: It's September 1st.
A: What day is it today?
B: It's Wednesday.

New Words

1. 请 qǐng v. (*polite*) please
*2. 问 wèn v. to ask, to inquire
3. 今天 jīntiān n. today
4. 号 hào n. (*for date of month*) number
5. 月 yuè n. month
6. 星期 xīngqī n. week

2 看日历 Look at the calendar 07-2

Zuótiān shì jǐ yuè jǐ hào?
A: 昨天 是 几 月几号?
Zuótiān shì bā yuè sānshíyī hào，xīngqī èr.
B: 昨天 是 8 月 31 号，星期 二。
Míngtiān ne?
A: 明天 呢?
Míngtiān shì jiǔ yuè èr hào，xīngqī sì.
B: 明天 是 9 月 2 号，星期 四。

English Version

A: What was the date yesterday?
B: It was Tuesday, August 31st.
A: What about tomorrow?
B: It's Thursday, September 2nd.

New Words

7. 昨天 zuótiān n. yesterday
8. 明天 míngtiān n. tomorrow

3 在咖啡馆儿 In a coffee house 07-3

Míngtiān xīngqī liù, nǐ qù xuéxiào ma?
A: 明天 星期 六，你去 学校 吗?
Wǒ qù xuéxiào.
B: 我 去学校。
Nǐ qù xuéxiào zuò shénme?
A: 你去学校 做 什么?
Wǒ qù xuéxiào kàn shū.
B: 我 去 学校 看 书。

English Version

A: Tomorrow is Saturday. Will you go to school?
B: Yes, I will.
A: What are you going to do there?
B: I'm going there to do some reading.

New Words

9. 去 qù v. to go
10. 学校 xuéxiào n. school
11. 看 kàn v. to look at, to watch, to read
12. 书 shū n. book

注释 Notes

1 日期的表达（1）：月、日（rì, date）/号、星期

Expression of a Date (1): month, date, day of the week

汉语的日期表达方式遵循由大到小的原则，先说“月”，然后说“日/号”，最后说“星期”。口语一般常用“号”。例如：

The way to say a date in Chinese observes the principle of “the bigger unit coming before the smaller one”. The month is said first, then the date and finally the day of the week. In spoken Chinese, “号” is often used instead of “日” to express the date. For example:

（1）9月1号，星期三。
（2）9月2号，星期四。
（3）8月31号，星期二。

2 名词谓语句 Sentences with a Nominal Predicate

名词谓语句是谓语部分由名词性成分充当的句子，一般用于表达年龄、时间、日期等。例如：

A sentence with a nominal predicate is a sentence whose predicate is a nominal element. It is usually used to indicate age, time, date and so on. For example:

Subject	Predicate
我的汉语老师	33岁。
明天	星期三。
今天	9月1号。

3 连动句（1）：去+地方+做什么

Sentences with a Serial Verb Construction (1): 去 + place + to do sth.

连动句的谓语部分由两个或者两个以上动词构成，后一个动作可以表示前一个动作的目的。第一个动词后表示地点的宾语有时可以省略。例如：

The predicate of a sentence with a serial verb construction consists of two or more verbs. The latter verb can be the purpose of the former. The object of the first verb, i.e. the place, can sometimes be omitted. For example:

Subject	Verb1		Verb2
	去	（place）	to do sth.
我	去	（中国）	学习汉语。
我们	去	（中国饭馆儿）	吃中国菜。
我	去	（学校）	看书。

练习 Exercises

1 分角色朗读课文 Role-play the dialogues.

2 朗读下列词语 Read the following words aloud.

yī yuè 一月 January	èr yuè 二月 February	sān yuè 三月 March	sì yuè 四月 April	wǔ yuè 五月 May	liù yuè 六月 June
qī yuè 七月 July	bā yuè 八月 August	jiǔ yuè 九月 September	shí yuè 十月 October	shíyī yuè 十一月 November	shí'èr yuè 十二月 December

xīngqī yī 星期一 Monday	xīngqī èr 星期二 Tuesday	xīngqī sān 星期三 Wednesday	xīngqī sì 星期四 Thursday
xīngqī wǔ 星期五 Friday	xīngqī liù 星期六 Saturday	xīngqīrì / xīngqītiān 星期日 / 星期天 Sunday	

3 根据实际情况回答问题 Answer the questions according to the actual situations.

1. 今天几月几号星期几？ Jīntiān jǐ yuè jǐ hào xīngqī jǐ?
2. 明天几月几号星期几？ Míngtiān jǐ yuè jǐ hào xīngqī jǐ?
3. 昨天几月几号星期几？ Zuótiān jǐ yuè jǐ hào xīngqī jǐ?
4. 明天你去哪儿做什么？ Míngtiān nǐ qù nǎr zuò shénme?
5. 星期日你去哪儿做什么？ Xīngqīrì nǐ qù nǎr zuò shénme?

4 用本课新学的语言点和词语描述图片

Describe the pictures using the newly-learned language points and words.

Jīntiān shì ______ yuè ______ hào,
今天是______月______号，
xīngqī
星期______。

Jīntiān ______ yuè ______ hào.
今天______月______号。

Èrshí'èr hào shì
22 号是______，
èrshísān hào shì
23 号是______。

Míngtiān wǒ qù ______ kàn ______.
明天 我去______看______。

拼音 Pinyin

双音节词语的声调搭配（2）：二声和各声调的搭配

Tone Collocation in Disyllabic Words (2): 2nd tone + 1st/2nd/3rd/4th tone

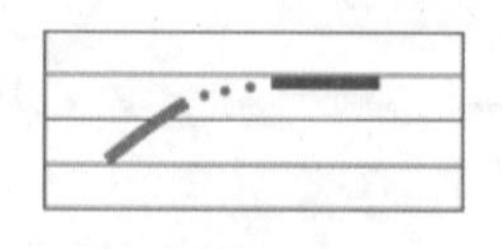
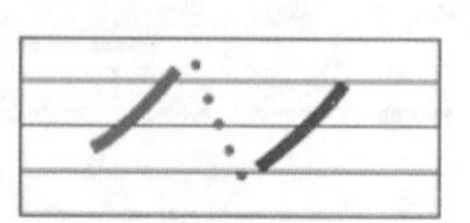

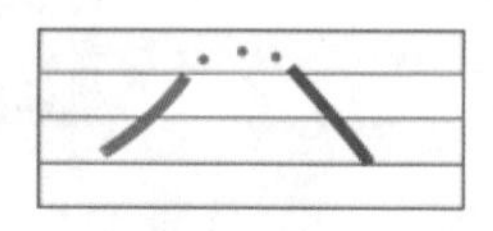

shíjiān 时间	yínháng 银行	cídiǎn 词典	lánsè 蓝色

听录音并跟读，注意声调的搭配 07-4

Listen to the recording and read after it. Pay attention to the collocation of tones.

guójiā	lóufáng	píngguǒ	huánjìng
zuótiān	lánqiú	píjiǔ	hánjià
míngtiān	míngnián	niúnǎi	niú ròu
niánqīng	Chángchéng	yóu yǒng	yóuxì

汉字 Characters

1 认识独体字 Single-Component Characters

（1）“四”，表示数量“4”。

“四” means “four”.

sì

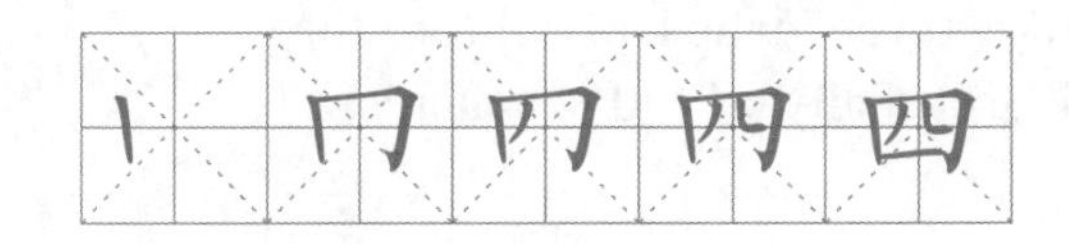

（2）“五”，表示数量“5”。

“五” means “five”.

wǔ

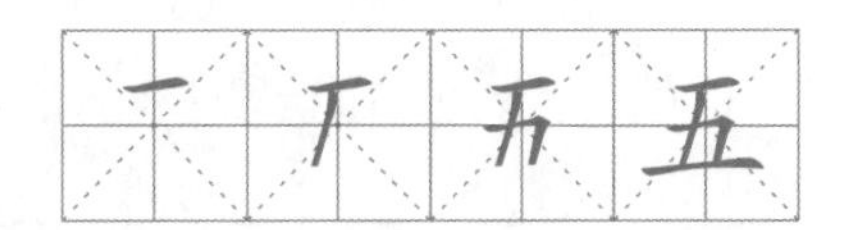

（3）“书”，本义是将毛笔放在墨池中蘸墨以便涂写，现在是“书写、书籍”等意思。

“书” originally meant “to dip the writing brush into the ink and write with it”, and now it means “writing” or “book”, etc.

shū

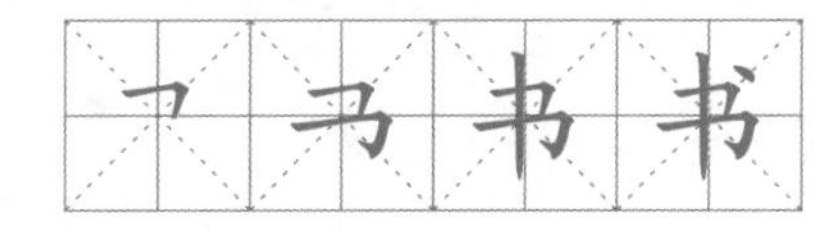

2 汉字结构（2）：左右结构与左中右结构

Structure of Chinese Characters (2): left-right and left-middle-right

合体结构中包括左右结构和左中右结构。左右结构的结构图形为⿰，左中右结构的图形为⿲。

Both the left-right structure and the left-middle-right structure are compound structures. The left-right structure is ⿰ and the left-middle-right structure is ⿲.

结构 Structure	例字 Example Characters	图解 Illustrations
左右结构 left-right	你 nǐ (*singular*) you 好 hǎo good, fine	你 好
左中右结构 left-middle-right	谢 xiè to thank 树 shù tree	谢 树

3 汉字偏旁"氵"和"讠" Chinese Radicals "氵" and "讠"

偏旁 Radical	解释 Explanation	例字 Example Characters
氵	三点水，一般和水有关系。 Shaped like three drops of water, the radical "氵" is usually related to water.	汉 hàn Chinese 没 méi to not have
讠	言字旁，一般和语言、说话有关系。 The radical "讠" is usually related to language and speech.	语 yǔ language 谁 shéi who, whom

运用 Application

1 双人活动 Pair Work

两人一组，根据实际情况进行问答练习。

Work in pairs and ask and answer questions according to the actual situatious.

例如：

Jīntiān shì jǐ yuè jǐ hào?
A: 今天是几月几号？
B: ……

Jīntiān xīngqī jǐ?
A: 今天星期几？
B: ……

Míngtiān shì jǐ yuè jǐ hào?
A: 明天是几月几号？
B: ……

Míngtiān xīngqī jǐ?
A: 明天星期几？
B: ……

Míngtiān nǐ zuò shénme?
A: 明天你做什么？
Míngtiān wǒ qù……
B: 明天我去……

2 小组活动 Group Work

3~4人一组，互相询问出生日期并记录，每组请一位同学报告情况。

Work in groups of 3-4. Ask about each other's birthdays and take notes. Each group chooses one member to make a report.

补充生词：生日 (shēngrì)

Supplementary word: birthday

	姓名 Name	生日 Birthday
1	李月 Lǐ Yuè	8月31号 bā yuè sānshíyī hào

8 我想喝茶

Wǒ xiǎng hē chá

I'd like some tea

热身 Warm-up

给下面的词语选择对应的图片

Match the pictures with the words/phrases.

A 

B 

C 

D 

E 

F 

qián ① 钱________	mǐfàn ② 米饭________	bēizi ③ 杯子________
chá ④ 茶________	Zhōngguó cài ⑤ 中国 菜________	Hànzì ⑥ 汉字________

课文 Text

1 在饭馆儿 In a restaurant 08-1

Nǐ xiǎng hē shénme?

A: 你 想 喝 什么?

Wǒ xiǎng hē chá.

B: 我 想 喝 茶。

Nǐ xiǎng chī shénme?

A: 你 想 吃 什么?

Wǒ xiǎng chī mǐfàn.

B: 我 想 吃 米饭。

English Version

A: What would you like to drink?

B: I'd like some tea.

A: What would you like to eat?

B: I'd like rice.

New Words

1. 想 xiǎng mod. to want, would like
2. 喝 hē v. to drink
3. 茶 chá n. tea
4. 吃 chī v. to eat
5. 米饭 mǐfàn n. cooked rice

2 在客厅 In the living room 08-2

Xiàwǔ nǐ xiǎng zuò shénme?
A: 下午你想 做 什么？
Xiàwǔ wǒ xiǎng qù shāngdiàn.
B: 下午 我 想 去 商店。
Nǐ xiǎng mǎi shénme?
A: 你 想 买 什么？
Wǒ xiǎng mǎi yí ge bēizi.
B: 我 想 买一个杯子。

English Version

A: What would you like to do this afternoon?
B: I'd like to go shopping.
A: What do you want to buy?
B: I want to buy a cup.

New Words

6. 下午 xiàwǔ n. afternoon
7. 商店 shāngdiàn n. shop, store
8. 买 mǎi v. to buy, to purchase
9. 个 gè m. *a general measure word*
10. 杯子 bēizi n. cup, glass

3 在商店 In a store 08-3

Nǐ hǎo! Zhège bēizi duōshao qián?
A: 你好！这个杯子 多少 钱？
Èrshíbā kuài.
B: 28 块。
Nàge bēizi duōshao qián?
A: 那个杯子 多少 钱？
Nàge bēizi shíbā kuài qián.
B: 那个杯子 18 块 钱。

English Version

A: Hello! How much is this cup?
B: 28 *yuan*.
A: What about that one?
B: That one is 18 *yuan*.

New Words

11. 这 zhè pron. this
12. 多少 duōshao pron. how many, how much
13. 钱 qián n. money
14. 块 kuài m. *a unit of money, same as "yuan"*
15. 那 nà pron. that

注释 Notes

1 能愿动词“想” The Modal Verb “想”

能愿动词“想”一般用在动词前表示一种希望或者打算。例如：

The modal verb “想” is usually used before a verb to express a hope or plan. For example:

（1）我想学汉语。

（2）明天我想去学校看书。

（3）我想买一个杯子。

2 疑问代词“多少” The Interrogative Pronoun “多少”

疑问代词“多少”用于询问十以上的数量，“多少”后边的量词可以省略。“多少”还用于询问价格，常用表达方式是“……多少钱？”。例如：

The interrogative pronoun “多少” is used to ask about numbers larger than 10. The measure word following it can be omitted. “多少” can also be used to inquire about prices, usually in the sentence pattern “……多少钱?”. For example:

（1）你们学校有多少（个）学生？

（2）你有多少（个）汉语老师？

（3）这个杯子多少钱？

3 量词“个”、“口” The Measure Words “个” and “口”

“个”是汉语中最常见的一个量词，一般用于没有专用量词的名词前。例如：

“个” is the most common measure word in Chinese, usually used before a noun without a specific measure word of its own. For example:

（1）三个老师

（2）五个学生

（3）一个杯子

“口”也是一个量词，一般用于描述家庭成员的人数（见第5课）。例如：

“口” is a measure word, too, usually used for members of a family(see Lesson 5). For example:

（1）李老师家有六口人。

（2）你家有几口人？

（3）我家有三口人。

4 钱数的表达 Expression of the Amount of Money

人民币的基本单位是“元”，口语中读作“块”。例如：

The basic unit of *Renminbi* (Chinese currency) is “元”, usually replaced by “块” in spoken Chinese. For example:

一元（块）
one *yuan/kuai*

五元（块）
five *yuan/kuai*

十元（块）
ten *yuan/kuai*

五十元（块）
fifty *yuan/kuai*

一百元（块）
one hundred *yuan/kuai*

练习 Exercises

1 分角色朗读课文 Role-play the dialogues.

2 根据实际情况回答问题 Answer the questions according to the actual situations.

1. 你想吃什么？ Nǐ xiǎng chī shénme?
2. 你想喝什么？ Nǐ xiǎng hē shénme?
3. 明天下午你想做什么？ Míngtiān xiàwǔ nǐ xiǎng zuò shénme?
4. 你去哪个商店买杯子？ Nǐ qù nǎge shāngdiàn mǎi bēizi?
5. 一个杯子多少钱？ Yí ge bēizi duōshao qián?

3 用本课新学的语言点和词语描述图片

Describe the pictures using the newly-learned language points and words.

Míngtiān ______ wǒ xiǎng qù ______ mǎi ______.
明天______我想去______买______。

Jīntiān wǒ xiǎng chī ______.
今天我想吃______。

Xiàwǔ wǒ xiǎng qù ______ kàn ______.
下午我想去______看______。

Nǐ hǎo, qǐngwèn zhège bēizi ______?
你好，请问这个杯子______？

拼音 Pinyin

双音节词语的声调搭配（3）：三声和各声调的搭配

Tone Collocation in Disyllabic Words (3): 3rd tone + $1^{st}/2^{nd}/3^{rd}/4^{th}$ tone

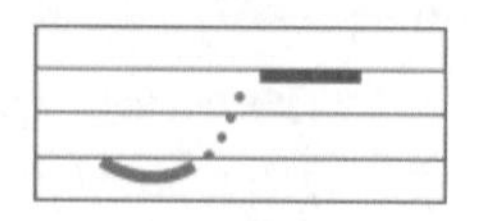

shǒujī
手机

shǒuzhuó
手镯

shǒubiǎo
手表

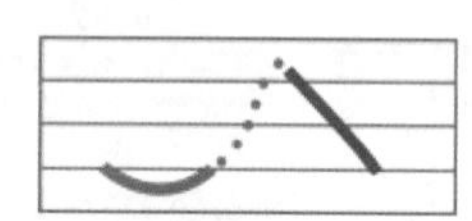

shǒutào
手套

听录音并跟读，注意声调的搭配 08-4

Listen to the recording and read after it. Pay attention to the collocation of tones.

lǎoshī	lǎorén	yǔsǎn	yǒu yòng
měi tiān	měi nián	měihǎo	měilì
hǎibiān	hǎimián	xǐ zǎo	gǎnxiè
yǐjīng	yǐqián	biǎoyǎn	biǎoxiàn

汉字 Characters

1 认识独体字 Single-Component Characters

（1）“少”，意思是规模小，数量不多，与“多”相对。

In contrast to “多(many)”, “少”means “few/little”, indicating a small scale or quantity.

shǎo

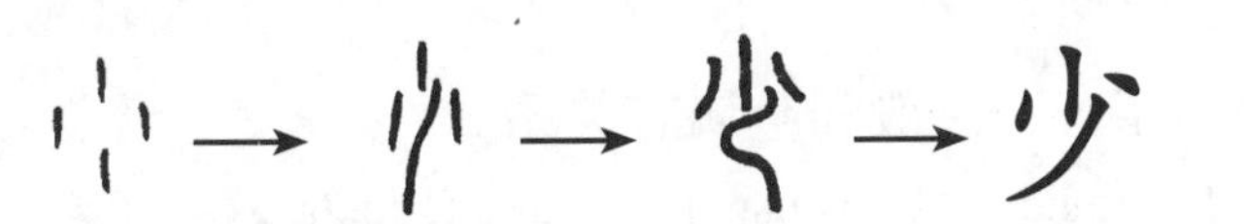

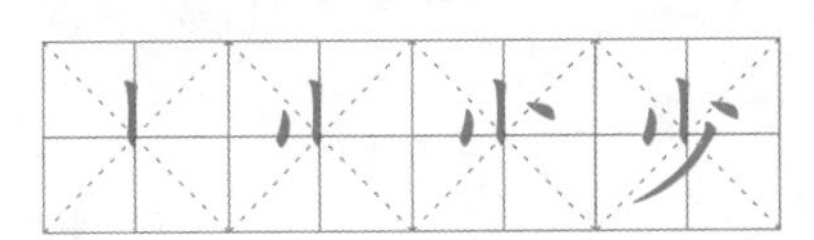

（2）“个”，本义是最小独立单位的人，指一个人。现在变为量词。

“个” originally meant “one individual person”. Now it has become a measure word.

gè

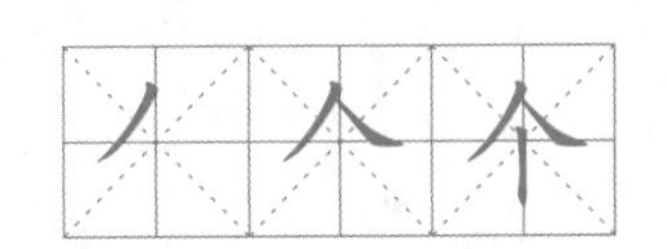

2 汉字结构（3）：上下结构与上中下结构

Structure of Chinese Characters (3): top-bottom and top-middle-bottom

合体结构还包括上下结构和上中下结构。上下结构的结构图形为⊟，上中下结构的图形为▤。

Both the top-bottom structure and the top-middle-bottom structure are compound structures. The top-bottom structure is ⊟ and the top-middle-bottom structure is ▤.

结构 Structure	例字 Example Characters	图解 Illustrations
上下结构 top-bottom	是 shì to be 爸 bà father	是 爸
上中下结构 top-middle-bottom	茶 chá tea 高 gāo high, tall	茶 高

3 汉字偏旁"钅"和"口" Chinese Radicals: "钅" and "口"

偏旁 Radical	解释 Explanation	例字 Example Characters
钅	金字旁，一般和金属有关系。 The radical "钅" is usually related to metal.	钟 zhōng clock 钱 qián money
口	口字旁，一般和嘴巴有关系。 The radical "口" is usually related to the mouth.	吃 chī to eat 喝 hē to drink

---

运用 Application

1 双人活动 Pair Work

两人一组，根据实际情况进行问答练习。

Work in pairs and ask and answer questions according to the actual situations.

例如：（1）A: 今天下午你想做什么？（Jīntiān xiàwǔ nǐ xiǎng zuò shénme?）

B: ……

A: 明天你想做什么？（Míngtiān nǐ xiǎng zuò shénme?）

B: ……

（2）A: 你们班有多少个学生？（Nǐmen bān yǒu duōshao ge xuésheng?）

B: ……

A: 你们学校有多少个老师？（Nǐmen xuéxiào yǒu duōshao ge lǎoshī?）

B: ……

2 小组活动 Group Work

3~4人一组，互相询问这个星期的计划并记录，每组请一位同学报告情况。

Work in groups of 3-4. Ask about each other's plan for the week and take notes. Each group chooses one member to make a report.

	姓名 Name	星期一 Monday	星期二 Tuesday	星期三 Wednesday	星期四 Thursday	星期五 Friday	星期六 Saturday	星期日 Sunday
1	谢朋 Xiè Péng	去学校 qù xuéxiào					去商店 qù shāngdiàn	

9 Nǐ érzi zài nǎr gōngzuò 你儿子在哪儿工作 Where does your son work

热身 Warm-up

给下面的词语选择对应的图片
Match the pictures with the words.

A

B

C
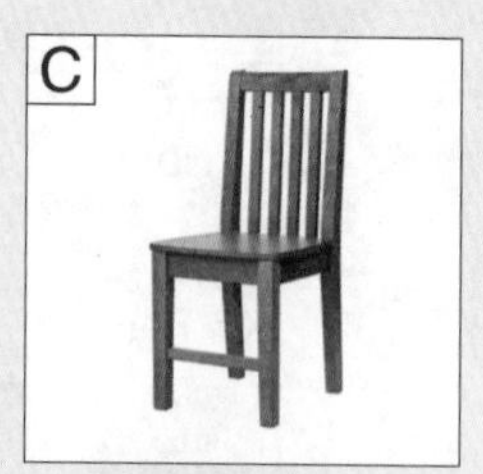
D
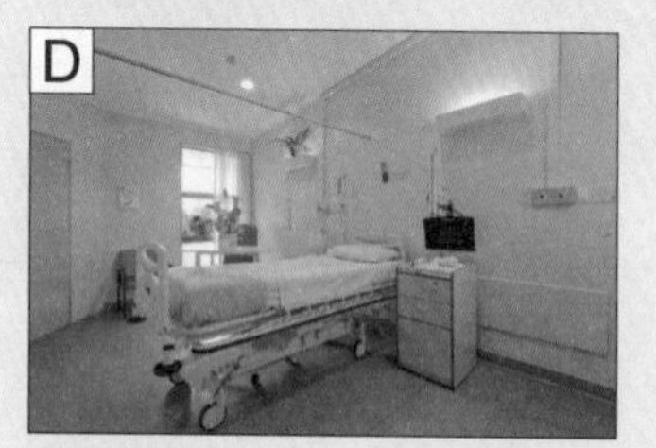
E

F

bàba ① 爸爸 ________	yīshēng ② 医生 ________	yīyuàn ③ 医院 ________
yǐzi ④ 椅子 ________	māo ⑤ 猫 ________	gǒu ⑥ 狗 ________

课文 Text

1 在家 At home 09-1

Xiǎo māo zài nǎr?
A: 小 猫 在 哪儿?

Xiǎo māo zài nàr.
B: 小 猫 在 那儿。

Xiǎo gǒu zài nǎr?
A: 小 狗 在 哪儿?

Xiǎo gǒu zài yǐzi xiàmiàn.
B: 小 狗 在 椅子 下面。

English Version

A: Where is the kitty?
B: The kitty is over there.
A: Where is the puppy?
B: The puppy is under the chair.

New Words

1. 小 xiǎo adj. small, little
2. 猫 māo n. cat
3. 在 zài v. to be in/on/at
4. 那儿 nàr pron. there
5. 狗 gǒu n. dog
6. 椅子 yǐzi n. chair
7. 下面（下） xiàmiàn(xià) n. under, below

2 在车站 At the railway station 09-2

Nǐ zài nǎr gōngzuò?
A: 你在哪儿工作？

Wǒ zài xuéxiào gōngzuò?
B: 我在学校工作。

Nǐ érzi zài nǎr gōngzuò?
A: 你儿子在哪儿工作？

Wǒ érzi zài yīyuàn gōngzuò，tā shì yīshēng.
B: 我儿子在医院工作，他是医生。

English Version

A: Where do you work?

B: I work in a school.

A: Where does your son work?

B: My son works in a hospital. He is a doctor.

New Words

8. 在 zài prep. in/on/at
9. 哪儿 nǎr pron. where
10. 工作 gōngzuò v./n. to work; job
11. 儿子 érzi n. son
12. 医院 yīyuàn n hospital
13. 医生 yīshēng n. doctor

3 打电话 On the phone 09-3

Nǐ bàba zài jiā ma?
A: 你爸爸在家吗？

Bú zài jiā.
B: 不在家。

Tā zài nǎr ne?
A: 他在哪儿呢？

Tā zài yīyuàn.
B: 他在医院。

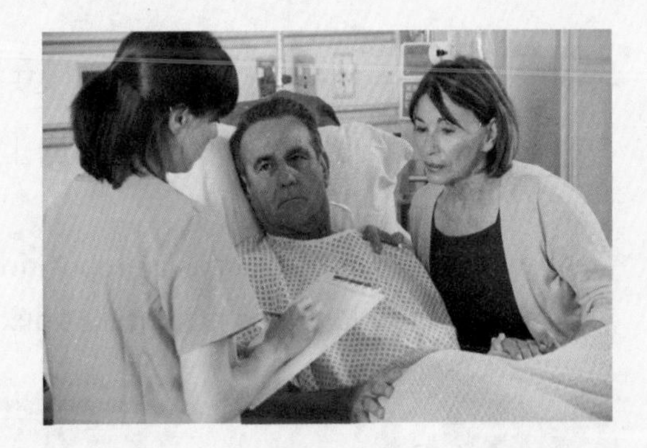

English Version

A: Is your father at home?

B: No, he isn't.

A: Where is he?

B: He is in the hospital.

New Word

14. 爸爸 bàba n. father

注释 Notes

1 动词“在” The Verb “在”

“在”是动词，后边加上表示位置的词语做句子的谓语，用于指示人或者事物的位置。例如：

“在” is a verb. When it is followed by a word of locality and acts as the predicate of a sentence, it indicates the location of somebody or something. For example:

Subject	Predicate	
	在	Word of Locality/Direction
我朋友	在	学校。
我妈妈	在	家。
小狗	在	椅子下面。

2 疑问代词“哪儿” The Interrogative Pronoun “哪儿”

疑问代词“哪儿”用于疑问句中，询问人或事物的位置。例如：

The interrogative pronoun “哪儿” is used to ask about the location of somebody or something. For example:

（1）我的杯子在哪儿？

（2）你的中国朋友在哪儿？

（3）小猫在哪儿？

3 介词“在” The Preposition “在”

“在”也是介词，后边加上表示位置的词语，用于介绍动作行为发生的位置。例如：

“在” can also act as a preposition, used before a word of locality to introduce the place where an action or behavior takes place. For example:

Subject	Predicate		
	在	Word of Locality/Direction	Verb
我	在	朋友家	喝茶。
他们	在	学校	看书。
我儿子	在	医院	工作。

4 疑问助词“呢”（2） The Interrogative Particle “呢” (2)

疑问助词“呢”用在句末，表示疑问，用于询问人或事物的位置。例如：

Used at the end of a sentence, the interrogative particle “呢” asks about the location of somebody or something. For example:

（1）我的小猫呢？

（2）我的杯子呢？

（3）他在哪儿呢？

练习 Exercises

1 分角色朗读课文 Role-play the dialogues.

2 根据课文内容回答问题。 Answer the questions based on the dialogues.

1. 小狗在哪儿？ Xiǎo gǒu zài nǎr?
2. 他在哪儿工作？ Tā zài nǎr gōngzuò?
3. 他儿子在哪儿工作？ Tā érzi zài nǎr gōngzuò?
4. 她爸爸在家吗？ Tā bàba zài jiā ma?
5. 她爸爸在哪儿呢？ Tā bàba zài nǎr ne?

3 用本课新学的语言点和词语描述图片

Describe the pictures using the newly-learned language points and words.

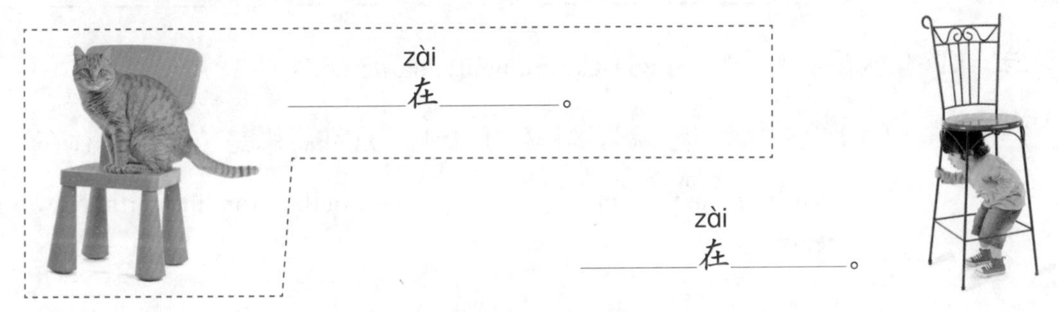

zài

_______在_______。

zài

_______在_______。

Wǒ māma shì　　　　tā zài

我妈妈是_______，她在_______。

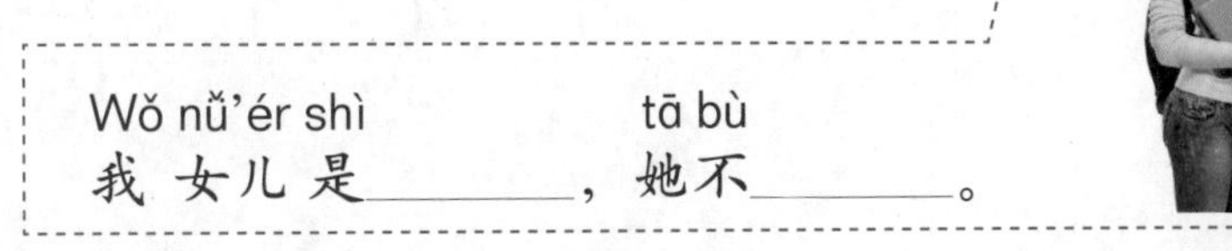

Wǒ nǚ'ér shì　　　　tā bù

我女儿是_______，她不_______。

拼音 Pinyin

双音节词语的声调搭配（4）：四声和各声调的搭配

Tone Collocation in Disyllabic Words (4): 4th tone + 1st/2nd/3rd/4th tone

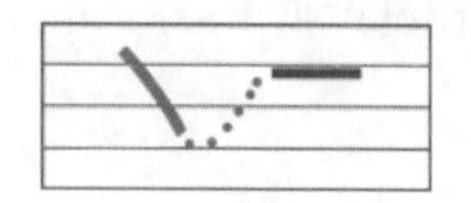
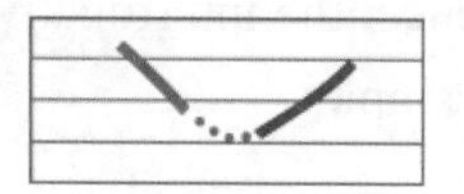

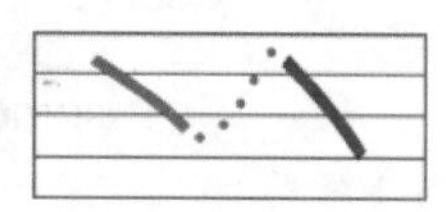

miànbāo 面包	miàntiáo 面条	diànnǎo 电脑	diànhuà 电话

听录音并跟读，注意声调的搭配 09-4

Listen to the recording and read after it. Pay attention to the collocation of tones.

xiàtiān	qùnián	tiào wǔ	shuì jiào
diàndēng	diànchí	diànyǐng	diànshì
chàng gē	fùxí	Hànyǔ	Hànzì
jiànkāng	dìtú	dìtiě	jiàn miàn

汉字 Characters

1 认识独体字 Single-Component Characters

（1）“在”，字形像草木初生于土上，现在意思是“存活、存在”。

The original form of “在” is like grass sprouting from the earth. Now it means “to live/exist”.

zài

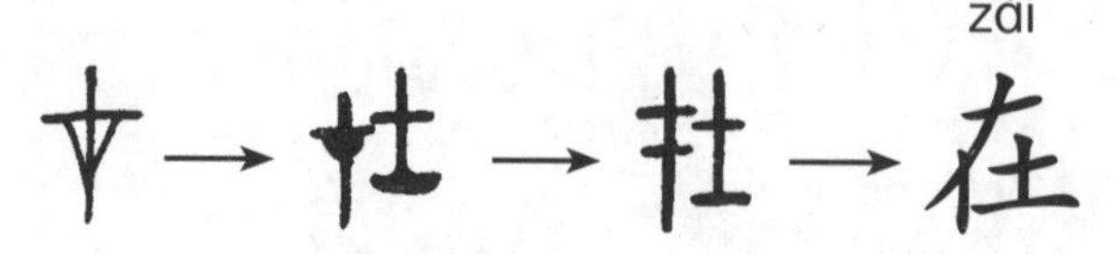

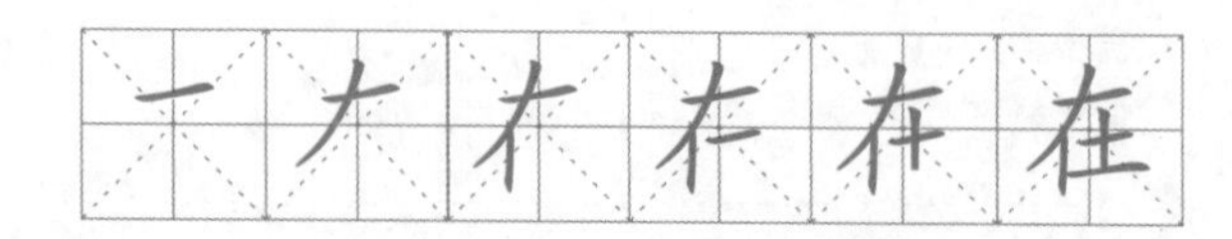

（2）“子”，本义是婴儿，现在意思很多，如“儿子”、“电子”。

“子” originally meant “baby”. Now it has many meanings, such as “儿子(son)” and “电子(electron)”.

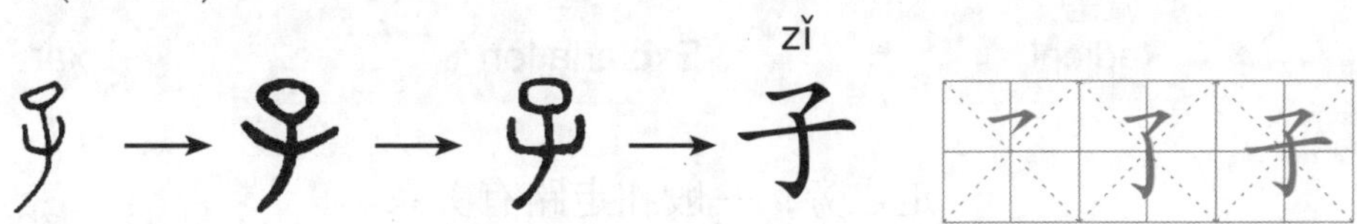

（3）“工”，字形像工匠的曲尺，现在意思很多，如“工人”、“工作”。

“工” was originally shaped like a craftsman's zigzag ruler. Now it has many meanings, such as “工人(worker)” and “工作(to work; job)”.

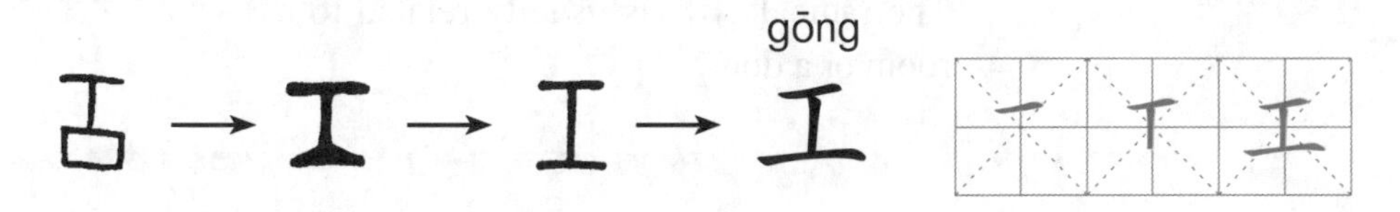

2 汉字结构（4）：半包围结构 Structure of Chinese Characters (4): half-enclosure

合体结构中还包括半包围结构和全包围结构（见第10课），本课的半包围结构又分为两面包围结构和三面包围结构。

There are another two kinds of compound structures—the half-enclosure structure and the enclosure structure (see Lesson 10). The half-enclosure structure in this lesson includes the structure enclosed by two sides and the structure enclosed by three sides.

结构 Structure	例字 Example Characters	图解 Illustrations
半包围结构 half-enclosure	店 diàn store 习 xí to study 这 zhè this 同 tóng same 凶 xiōng fierce 医 yī doctor	店 习 这 同 凶 医

3 汉字偏旁“辶”和“门” Chinese Radicals: “辶” and “门”

偏旁 Radical	解释 Explanation	例字 Example Characters
辶	走之旁，一般和走路有关系。 The radical “辶” is usually related to “walking”.	这 zhè this 送 sòng to send
门	门字框，一般和房间、房门有关。 The radical “门” is usually related to a room or a door.	问 wèn to ask 间 jiān *a measure word for rooms*

运用 Application

1 双人活动 Pair Work

两人一组，根据实际情况进行问答练习。

Work in pairs and ask and answer questions according to the actual situations.

例如：（1）A: ……在哪儿？(zài nǎr?)

B: ……在……(zài)

（2）A: ……在哪儿工作？(zài nǎr gōngzuò?)

B: ……在……工作，他/她是……(zài gōngzuò, tā / tā shì)

2 小组活动 Group Work

3~4人一组，互相介绍自己的朋友、同学的工作情况并记录，每组请一位同学报告情况。

Work in groups of 3-4. Tell each other about the jobs of your friends or classmates and take notes. Each group chooses one member to make a report.

	朋友/同学 Friend/Classmate	工作 Job
1	李朋 Lǐ Péng	是医生，在医院工作。Shì yīshēng，zài yīyuàn gōngzuò.

10 Wǒ néng zuò zhèr ma 我能坐这儿吗 Can I sit here

热身 Warm-up

给下面的词语选择对应的图片

Match the pictures with the words/phrases.

A 

B 

C 

D 

E 

F 

① gōngzuò 工作______	② kàn shū 看书______	③ zuò 坐______
④ zhuōzi 桌子______	⑤ diànnǎo 电脑______	⑥ bàba hé māma 爸爸和妈妈______

课文 Text

1 在办公室 In the office 10-1

Zhuōzi shang yǒu shénme?
A: 桌子 上 有 什么?

Zhuōzi shang yǒu yí ge diànnǎo hé yì běn shū.
B: 桌子 上 有一个 电脑 和一本 书。

Bēizi zài nǎr?
A: 杯子在哪儿?

Bēizi zài zhuōzi li.
B: 杯子在桌子里。

English Version

A: What are there on the desk?
B: There is a computer and a book.
A: Where is the cup?
B: It's in the desk.

New Words

1. 桌子 zhuōzi n. desk, table
2. 上 shang n. up, above
3. 电脑 diànnǎo n. computer
4. 和 hé conj. and
5. 本 běn m. *a measure word for books*
6. 里 li n. inner, inside, interior

2 在健身房 In the gym 10-2

Qiánmiàn nàge rén jiào shénme míngzi?
A: 前面 那个人叫 什么 名字?

Tā jiào Wáng Fāng，zài yīyuàn gōngzuò.
B: 她叫 王 方，在医院 工作。

Hòumiàn nàge rén ne? Tā jiào shénme míngzi?
A: 后面 那个人呢? 他叫 什么 名字?

Tā jiào Xiè Péng，zài shāngdiàn gōngzuò.
B: 他叫谢 朋，在 商店 工作。

English Version

A: Who is the person in the front?
B: She is Wang Fang. She works in a hospital.
A: What about the person at the back? What's his name?
B: He is Xie Peng. He works in a store.

New Words

7. 前面 qiánmiàn n. front
8. 后面 hòumiàn n. back

Proper Nouns

1. 王方 Wáng Fāng Wang Fang, name of a person
2. 谢朋 Xiè Péng Xie Peng, name of a person

3 在图书馆 In the library 10-3

Zhèr yǒu rén ma?
A: 这儿有 人 吗?

Méi yǒu.
B: 没 有。

Wǒ néng zuò zhèr ma?
A: 我 能 坐这儿吗?

Qǐng zuò.
B: 请 坐。

English Version

A: Is this seat taken?
B: No, it isn't.
A: Can I sit here?
B: Yes, please.

New Words

9. 这儿 zhèr pron. here
10. 没有（没） méiyǒu (méi) adv. there is not
11. 能 néng mod. can, may
12. 坐 zuò v. to sit, to be seated

注释 Notes

1 "有"字句：表示存在 The "有" Sentence: indicating existence

动词"有"可以用于表示存在的句子中，表示某个处所或者位置存在什么。例如：

The verb "有" can be used in an existential sentence to indicate a person or thing exists somewhere. For example:

Word of Locality	有	Person/Thing Existing
椅子下面	有	一只小狗。
学校里	有	一个商店。
桌子上	有	一个电脑和一本书。

"有"字句的否定形式是"没有"，同时宾语前不能带数量定语。例如：

In the negative form of a "有" sentence, "没有" is used without a numeral classifier before the object. For example:

（1）椅子下面没有小狗。

（2）学校里没有商店。

（3）桌子上没有电脑和书。

2 连词"和" The Conjunction "和"

连词"和"用于连接两个或者两个以上并列的成分，表示一种并列关系。例如：

The conjunction "和" is used to connect two or more elements, indicating a parallel relationship. For example:

（1）我有一个中国朋友和一个美国朋友。

（2）我家有三口人，爸爸、妈妈和我。

（3）桌子上有一个电脑和一本书。

3 能愿动词"能" The Modal Verb "能"

能愿动词"能"一般用在动词前，与动词整体做谓语，表示一种能力或者可能。"能"还常用于疑问句式"能……吗？"中，表示请求、希望获得许可。例如：

The modal verb "能" is usually used before a verb to form the predicate indicating an ability or a possibility. The interrogative sentence structure "能……吗?" is often used to indicate a request or hope for permission. For example:

（1）明天下午我能去商店。

（2）你能在这儿写你的名字吗？

（3）我能坐这儿吗？

4 用“请”的祈使句 Imperative Sentences with “请”

动词“请”后加其他动词可以构成一种祈使句，委婉地表示建议、希望对方做某事。例如：

When the verb “请” is used before another verb, an imperative sentence is formed, indicating a polite suggestion or hope. For example:

（1）请写您的名字。

（2）请喝茶。

（3）请坐。

练习 Exercises

1 分角色朗读课文 Role-play the dialogues.

2 根据课文内容回答问题 Answer the questions based on the dialogues.

1. 电脑在哪儿？ Diànnǎo zài nǎr?
2. 书在哪儿？ Shū zài nǎr?
3. 桌子里面有什么？ Zhuōzi lǐmiàn yǒu shénme?
4. 哪个人是王方？ Nǎge rén shì Wáng Fāng?
5. 哪个人是谢朋？ Nǎge rén shì Xiè Péng?

3 用本课新学的语言点和词语描述图片

Describe the pictures using the newly-learned language points and words.

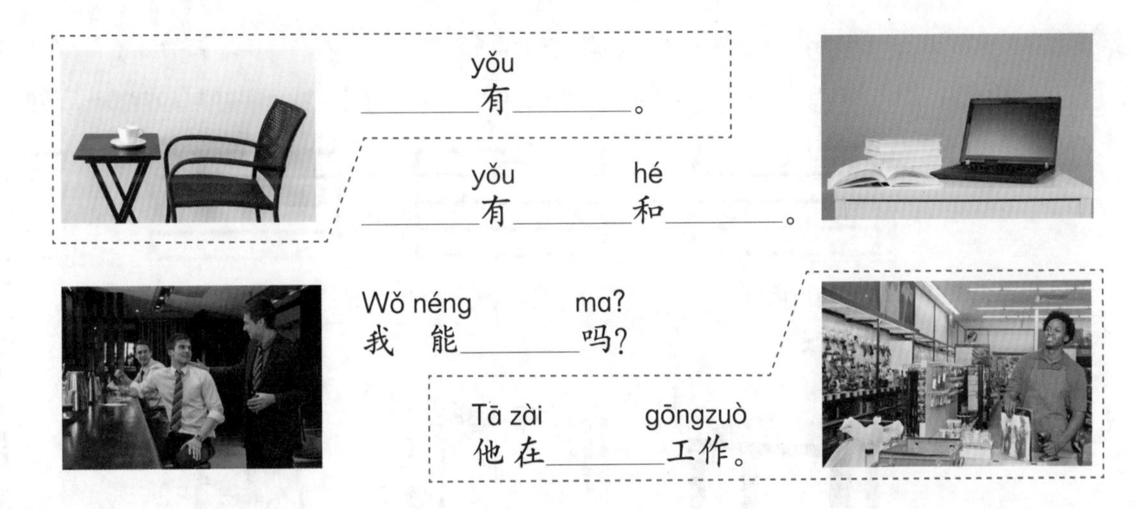

4 选择适当的量词填空 Choose a suitable measure word to fill in each blank.

gè 个	kǒu 口	běn 本	kuài 块

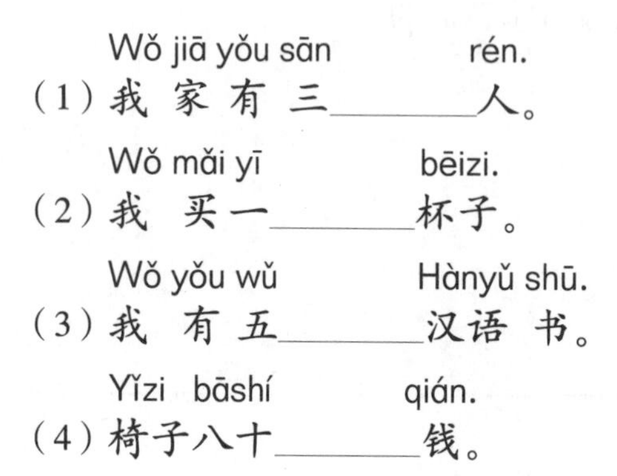

Wǒ jiā yǒu sān ______ rén.
（1）我 家 有 三______人。

Wǒ mǎi yī ______ bēizi.
（2）我 买 一______杯子。

Wǒ yǒu wǔ ______ Hànyǔ shū.
（3）我 有 五______汉语 书。

Yǐzi bāshí ______ qián.
（4）椅子八十______钱。

拼音 Pinyin

1 轻声音节的读法 Pronunciation of Neutral-Tone Syllables 10-4

轻声音节的实际发音是由前一个音节的音高决定的。轻声的读法，一般来说是在第一声、第二声、第四声后面读的调子比前一个音节低一些，而第三声后面的轻声比前面的音节高一些。

The actual pronunciation of a neutral-tone syllable depends upon the pitch of the syllable before it. Generally speaking, a neutral-tone syllable is read in a lower pitch than the syllable before it if it follows a first-tone, second-tone or fourth-tone syllable, but when it follows a third-tone syllable, it is read in a higher pitch than the syllable before it.

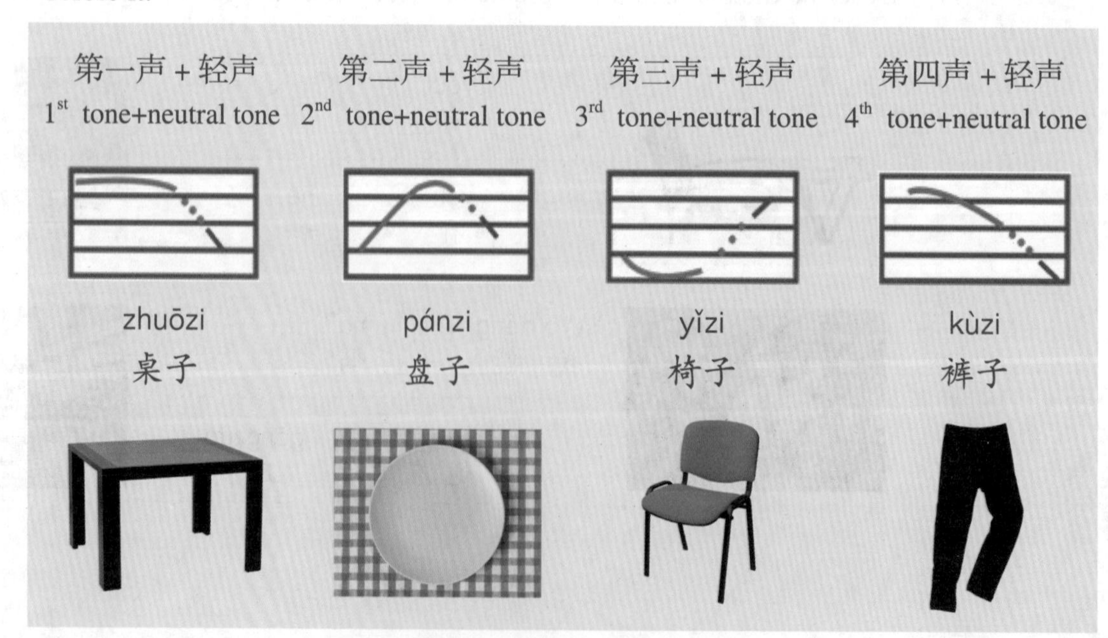

2 叠音词的读法 Pronunciation of Reduplicated Syllables

在双音节的叠音词中，后一个音节大多读作轻声。

In a disyllabic word with reduplicated syllables, the second syllable is usually read in the neutral tone.

听录音并跟读，注意轻声音节的读法 10-5

Listen to the recording and read after it. Pay attention to the neutral tone.

bàba	māma	yéye	nǎinai
gēge	jiějie	dìdi	mèimei
gūgu	shūshu	tàitai	xīngxing
xièxie	kànkan	shuōshuo	chángchang

3 带后缀词的读法："-们，-子，-头"

Pronunciation of Words with the Suffix "-们", "-子" or "-头"

在带后缀"-们、-子、-头"的词语中，"们、子、头"一般读作轻声。例如：

Being part of a word, the suffixes "们", "子" and "头" are usually read in the neutral tone. For example:

听录音并跟读，注意后缀的读法 10-6

Listen to the recording and read after it. Pay attention to the suffixes.

nǐmen 你们	wǒmen 我们	tāmen 他们	rénmen 人们
zhuōzi 桌子	yǐzi 椅子	bēizi 杯子	bèizi 被子
shétou 舌头	zhěntou 枕头	shítou 石头	mùtou 木头
qiántou 前头	hòutou 后头	lǐtou 里头	wàitou 外头

汉字 Characters

1 认识独体字 Single-Component Characters

（1）“上”，下边的横表示位置的界线，上边的短横表示在上面。意思是“高处、上面”。

The horizontal stroke at the bottom of “上” indicates the border line for reference, and the short horizontal stroke indicates a position above the border line, meaning “up/above”.

shàng

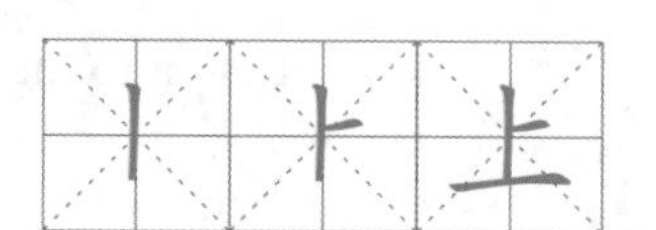

（2）“下”，与“上”的意思相对，指位置在低处、下面。

Opposite to “上”, “下” means “down/below”.

xià

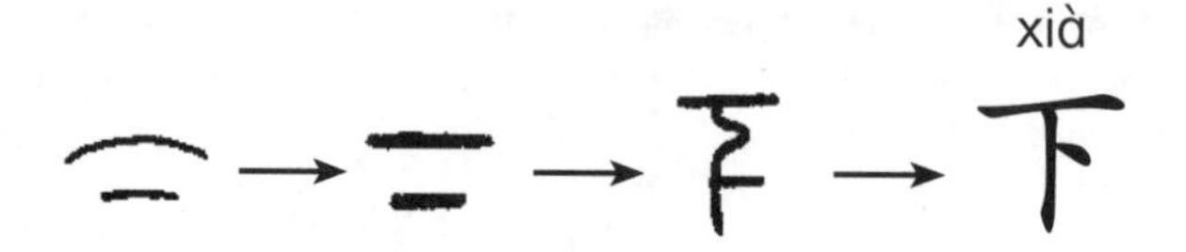

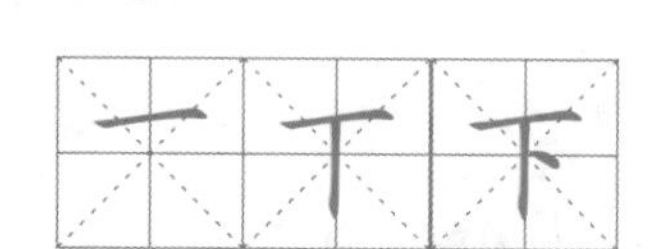

（3）“本”，字形是在“木”的下端加圆点指事符号·，本义是指树的根部，后引申为事物的根本。

“本” originally looked like a tree with a dot sign at its bottom. The character originally referred to the root of a tree, and now it means “the root of everything”.

běn

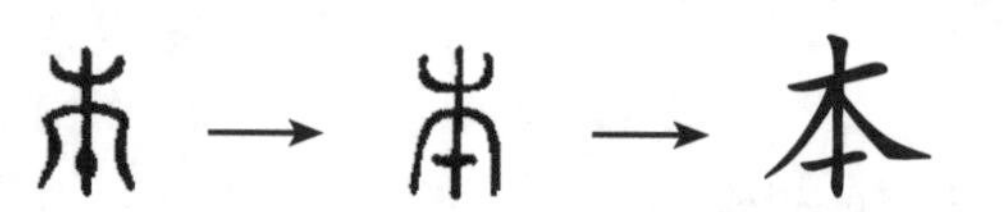

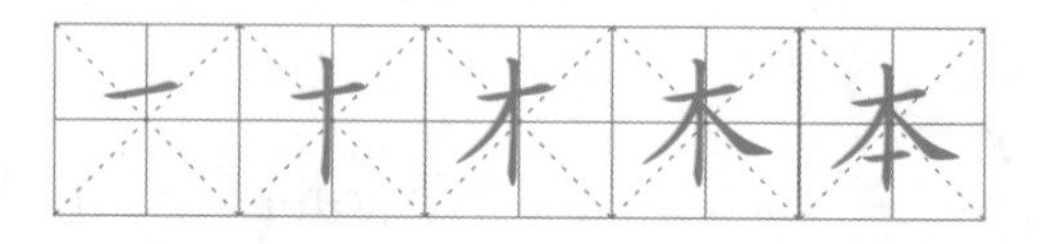

（4）“末”，本义是树梢部位、尖端，现在也指非根本的、次要的。

“末” originally referred to the tip or top of a tree. Now it also means “non-fundamental and secondary”.

mò

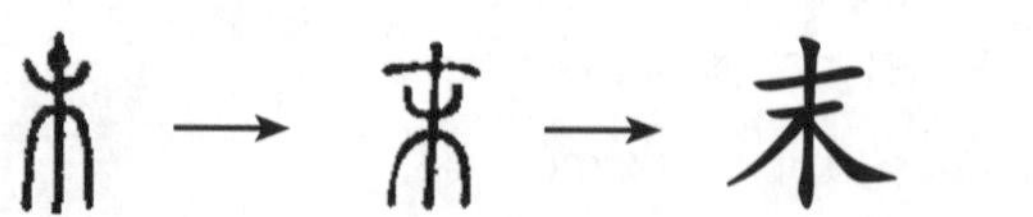

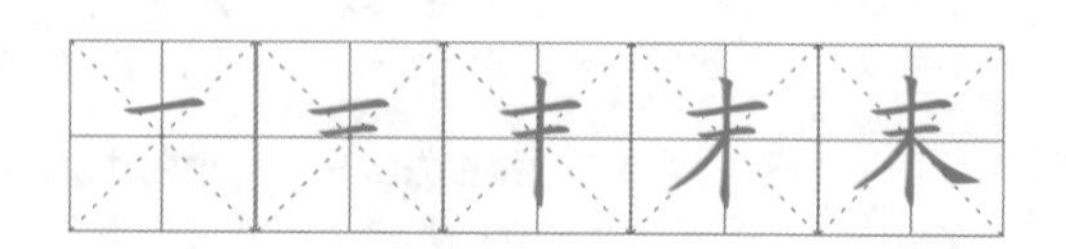

2 汉字结构（5）：全包围结构 Structure of Chinese Characters (5): enclosure

合体结构中的全包围结构是指四面包围结构，结构图形为□。

As a compound structure, the enclosure structure is a structure enclosed on all the four sides. The diagram is □.

结构 Structure	例字 Example Characters	图解 Illustrations
全包围结构 complete enclosure	四 sì four 国 guó country, nation	四 国

3 汉字偏旁“口”和“礻” Chinese Radicals: “口” and “礻”

偏旁 Radical	解释 Explanation	例字 Example Characters
口	国字框，一般表示被困住、包围住。 The radical “口” usually means being trapped or besieged.	国 guó country, nation 困 kùn to be trapped
礻	示字旁，是“示”的变体，一般和神、祭祀、福祸有关。 The radical “礻” is a variant of “示”, a character usually related to deity, sacrificial rites and one's fortune.	视 shì to look, to view 祝 zhù to wish

运用 Application

1 双人活动 Pair Work

两人一组，根据实际情况进行问答练习。

Work in pairs and ask and answer questions according to the actual situations.

例如：A: Nǐ de zhuōzi shàngmiàn yǒu shénme?
你的桌子上面有什么？

B: ……

A: Nǐ de yǐzi xiàmiàn yǒu shénme?
你的椅子下面有什么？

B: ……

2 小组活动 Group Work

3~4人一组，互相介绍小组各成员的座位位置并记录，每组请一位同学报告情况。

Work in groups of 3-4. Describe the location of the seat of each of your group member and take notes. Each group chooses one member to make a report.

补充生词：后面 hòumiàn、左边 zuǒbian、右边 yòubian

Supplementary words: behind, left, right

	姓名 Name	位置 Location
1	大卫 Dàwèi	大卫在我左边。/我左边是大卫。 Dàwèi zài wǒ zuǒbian./ Wǒ zuǒbian shì Dàwèi.

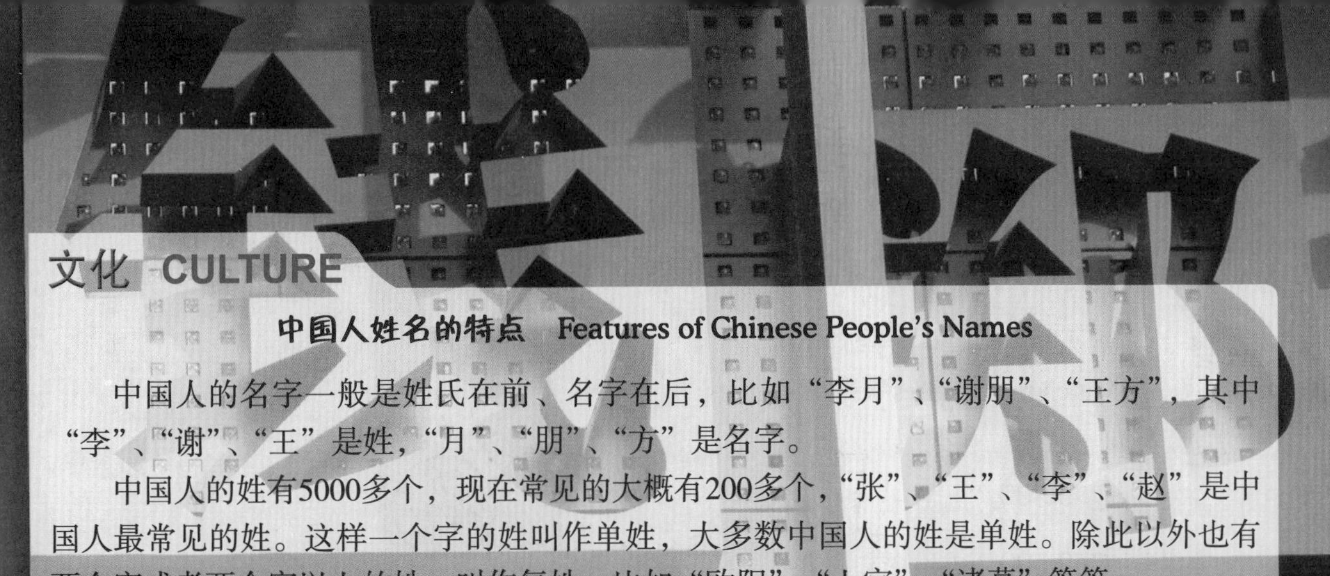

文化 CULTURE

中国人姓名的特点　Features of Chinese People's Names

中国人的名字一般是姓氏在前、名字在后，比如"李月"、"谢朋"、"王方"，其中"李"、"谢"、"王"是姓，"月"、"朋"、"方"是名字。

中国人的姓有5000多个，现在常见的大概有200多个，"张"、"王"、"李"、"赵"是中国人最常见的姓。这样一个字的姓叫作单姓，大多数中国人的姓是单姓。除此以外也有两个字或者两个字以上的姓，叫作复姓，比如"欧阳"、"上官"、"诸葛"等等。

在称呼时，可以用一个人的姓加上这个人的工作或者职业。比如，李月姓李，是老师，我们可以称呼她"李老师"；王方姓王，是医生，我们可以称呼她"王医生"。

A Chinese name starts with the family name and ends with the given name, for example, in the names "李月", "谢朋" and "王方", "李", "谢" and "王" are family names and "月", "朋" and "方" are given names.

There are over 5,000 Chinese family names, among which more than 200 are commonly seen. "张", "王", "李" and "赵" are the most common ones. Such family names as have only one character are known as single-character surnames. Most Chinese people have a single-character surname. There are surnames with two or more characters also, which are called compound-character surnames, such as "欧阳", "上官" and "诸葛".

A person can be addressed with his/her family name followed by his/her job or profession. For instance, "李月" is a teacher, so we can call her "李老师" (literally Teacher Li), while "王方" is a doctor and we can call her "王医生" (literally Doctor Wang).

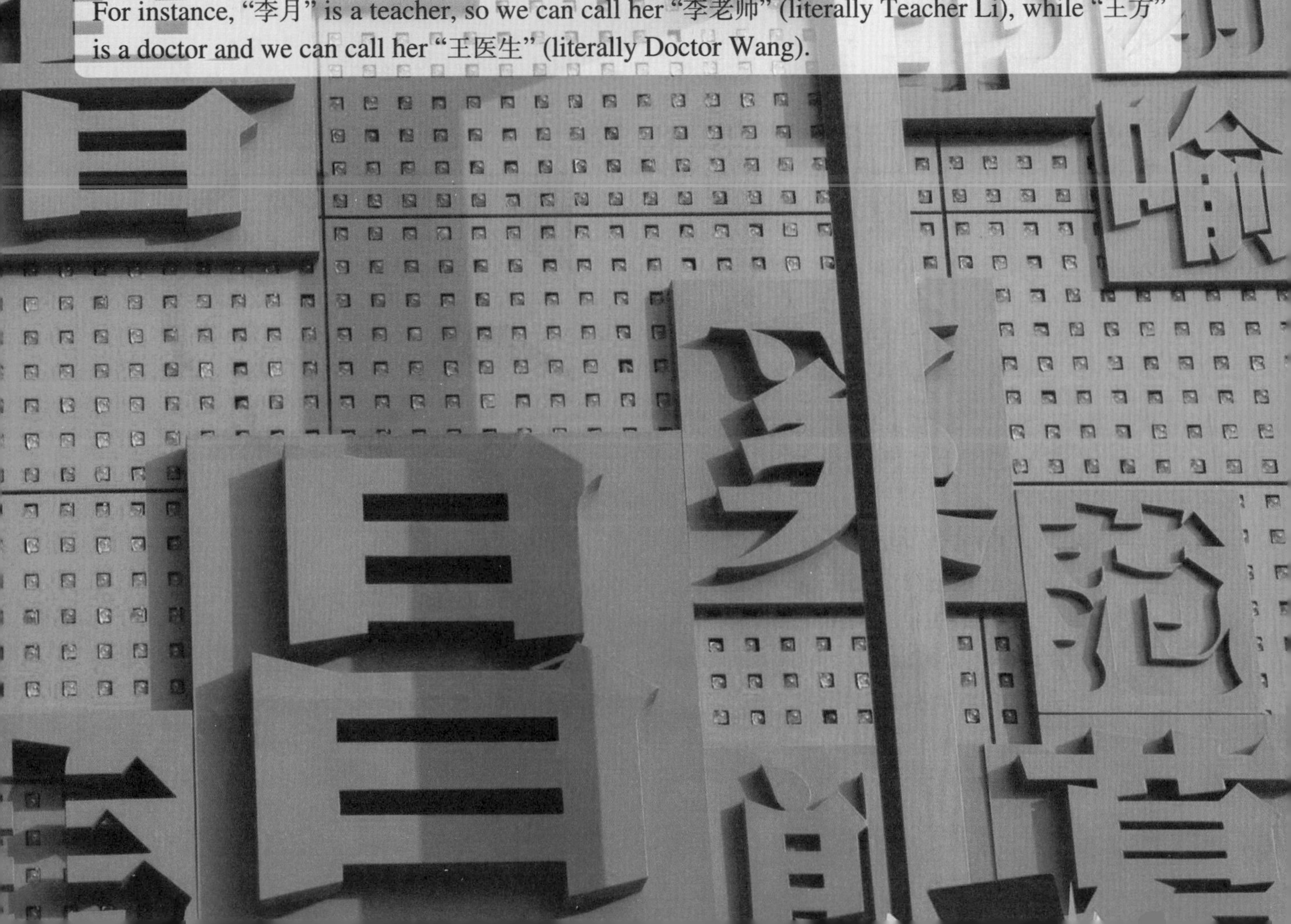

11 Xiànzài jǐ diǎn 现在几点 What's the time now

热身 Warm-up

给下面的词语选择对应的时间

Match the pictures with the times.

❶ 5: 00________

❷ 2: 00________

❸ 9: 45________

❹ 12: 00________

❺ 3: 05________

❻ 6: 30________

❼ 10: 10________

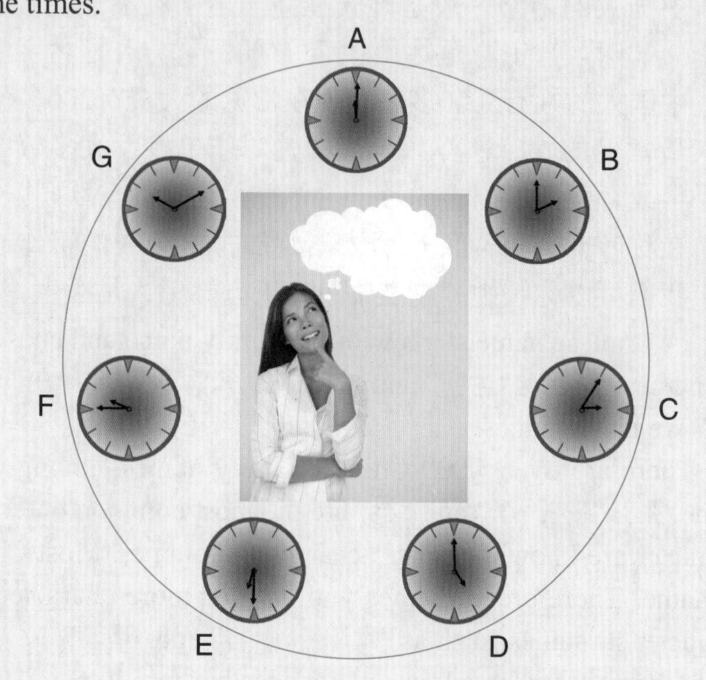

课文 Text

1 在图书馆 In the library 11-1

Xiànzài jǐ diǎn?
A: 现在 几 点？

Xiànzài shí diǎn shí fēn.
B: 现在 十 点 十 分。

Zhōngwǔ jǐ diǎn chī fàn?
A: 中午 几点 吃 饭？

Shí'èr diǎn chī fàn.
B: 十二 点 吃 饭。

English Version

A: What's the time now?
B: It's ten past ten.
A: When shall we have our lunch?
B: At twelve o'clock.

New Words

1. 现在 xiànzài n. now
2. 点 diǎn m. o'clock
3. 分 fēn m. minute
4. 中午 zhōngwǔ n. noon
5. 吃饭 chī fàn v. to eat a meal

2 在家 At home 11-2

Bàba shénme shíhou huí jiā?
A: 爸爸 什么 时候 回家?
Xiàwǔ wǔ diǎn.
B: 下午 五 点。
Wǒmen shénme shíhou qù kàn diànyǐng?
A: 我们 什么 时候 去 看 电影?
Liù diǎn sānshí fēn.
B: 六 点 三十 分。

English Version

A: When is father coming home?
B: At five o'clock in the afternoon.
A: When are we going to see the movie?
B: At half past six.

New Words

6. 时候 shíhou n. time, moment
7. 回 huí v. to come/go back, to return
8. 我们 wǒmen pron. we, us
9. 电影 diànyǐng n. film, movie

3 在家 At home 11-3

Wǒ xīngqī yī qù Běijīng.
A: 我 星期一 去 北京。
Nǐ xiǎng zài Běijīng zhù jǐ tiān?
B: 你 想 在 北京 住 几 天?
Zhù sān tiān.
A: 住 三 天。
Xīngqī wǔ qián néng huí jiā ma?
B: 星期 五 前 能 回家 吗?
Néng.
A: 能。

English Version

A: I'll go to Beijing next Monday.
B: How long will you stay in Beijing?
A: For three days.
B: Can you come back before Friday?
A: Yes, I can.

New Words

10. 住 zhù v. to live, to stay
11. 前 qián n. before, earlier than

Proper Noun

北京 Běijīng Beijing, capital of China

注释 Notes

1 时间的表达 Expression of Time

（1）汉语表达时间的时候要用“点”、“分”，遵循由大到小的顺序。

“点” and “分” are used to express time in Chinese, observing the principle of “the bigger unit preceding the smaller unit”.

用“点”来表示整点。例如：

“点” means “o’clock”, indicating a whole hour. For example:

9:00 → 九点
11:00 → 十一点
2:00 → 两点（liǎng diǎn）

*注意：在表达 2 o’clock时，我们说两点（liǎng diǎn），不说二点（èr diǎn）。
Note: The counterpart of 2 o’clock in Chinese is “两点 (liǎng diǎn)” instead of “二点 (èr diǎn)”.

当不是整点的时候要用到“分”，格式是“……点……分”。例如：

If it is not a “whole-hour” time, “分” is used. The pattern is “……点……分”. For example:

5:30 → 五点三十分
11:10 → 十一点十分
2:05 → 两点零（líng，zero）五分

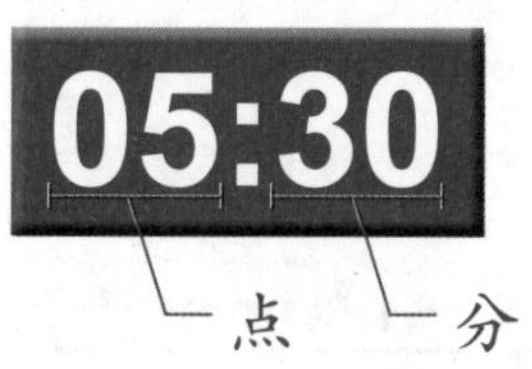

（2）如果区分上午或者下午，一般格式是“上午……点（……分），下午……点（……分）”。例如：

To distinguish a time before noon from one afternoon, the pattern “上午 (morning)……点（……分）” or “下午 (afternoon)……点（……分）” is used. For example:

8:00 am → 上午八点
3:10 pm → 下午三点十分
5:25 pm → 下午五点二十五分

2 时间词做状语 Time Word Used as an Adverbial

时间词在句子中做状语，经常出现在主语后边，也可以在主语前边。例如：

When a time word serves as an adverbial modifier in a sentence, it often follows the subject. Sometimes it can be used before the subject. For example:

Subject	Time（adverbial）	Predicate
妈妈	六点	做饭。
李老师	上午八点	去学校。
我	星期一	去北京。

Time (adverbial)	Subject	Predicate
七点	我	吃饭。
中午十二点	我们	回家。
下午五点	他们	去看电影。

3 名词“前” The Noun “前”

名词“前”可以表示现在或者所说的某个时间以前的时间。例如：

The noun “前” can be used to refer to a period prior to the present time or the time being mentioned. For example:

(1) 三天前　一个星期前　四点前　星期五前

(2) A: 你什么时候去学校？

B: 八点前。

(3) A: 你什么时候回北京？

B: 星期六前。

(4) A:（你）星期五前能回家吗？

B: 能。

练习 Exercises

1 分角色朗读课文 Role-play the dialogues.

2 根据课文内容回答问题 Answer the questions based on the dialogues.

1. 现在几点？Xiànzài jǐ diǎn?
2. 他们几点吃饭？Tāmen jǐ diǎn chī fàn?
3. 爸爸什么时候回家？Bàba shénme shíhou huí jiā?
4. 他们什么时候去看电影？Tāmen shénme shíhou qù kàn diànyǐng?
5. 他去哪儿？什么时候能回家？Tā qù nǎr? Shénme shíhou néng huí jiā?

3 用本课新学的语言点和词语描述图片

Describe the pictures using the newly-learned language points and words.

Tā　　　zài xuéxiào
她______在 学校______。

Wáng Fāng zhōngwǔ　　　qù
王　方　中午______去
shāngdiàn
商店______。

Tāmen hěn máng,　　xīngqī liù
他们 很 忙(busy)，星期 六______
yě gōngzuò.
也 工作。

Tā shàngwǔ bù hē chá，xiàwǔ　　　qián hē chá.
她 上午 不喝 茶，下午______前 喝 茶。

拼音 Pinyin　轻声的功能　Function of Neutral-Tone Syllables

11-4

汉语中轻声不仅是一种音变现象，而且还能区分词义。比如：东西，读作“dōngxī”指方向，读作“dōngxi”指物品。

The neutral tone in Chinese is not only a phonological phenomenon, but also a way to distinguish meanings. For example, the word “东西” refers to the directions east and west when read as “dōngxī”, but when read as “dōngxi”, it means “thing/stuff”.

老子	lǎozi (*slang*) father (n.)	Lǎozǐ Lao-tzu, an ancient Chinese thinker (p.n.)
买卖	mǎimai business (n.)	mǎimài to buy and sell (v.)
大意	dàyi careless (adj.)	dàyì rough idea (n.)

汉字 Characters

1 认识独体字 Single-Component Characters

（1）“午”，表示一天中白天十一点到一点的一段时间。

“午” in Chinese refers to the period of time between 11 am and 1 pm.

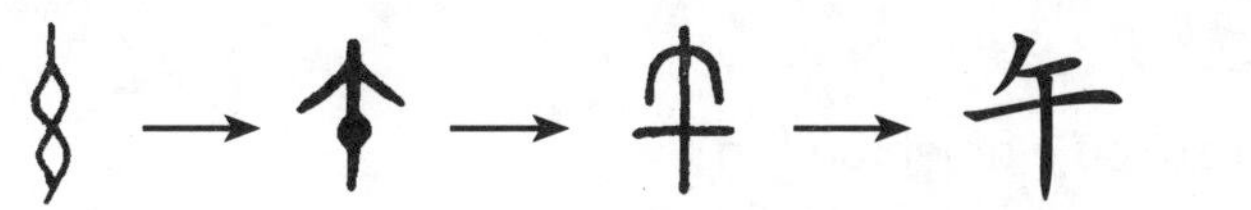

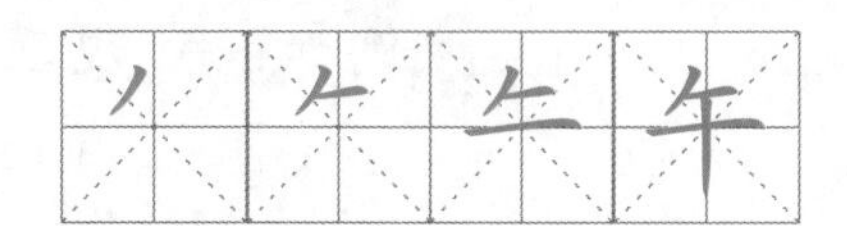

（2）“电”，本义是下雨时天上出现的锋利多齿的闪光，是一种物理现象，也是一种能源。

“电” originally referred to a sharp and multi-edged flash in the sky during a rain. It is both a physical phenomenon and a type of energy.

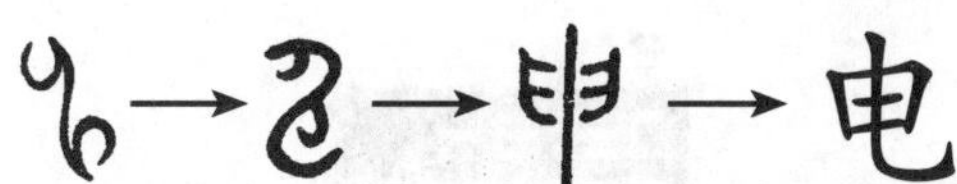

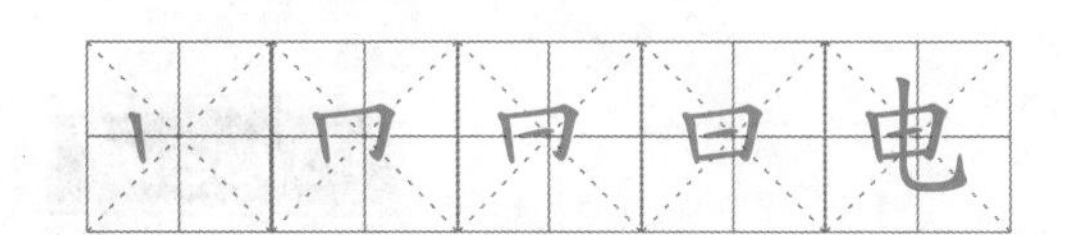

2 汉字偏旁“阝”和“亻” Chinese Radicals: “阝” and “亻”

偏旁 Radical	解释 Explanation	例字 Example Characters
阝	耳刀旁，一般跟地形、位置有关系。 The radical “阝” is usually related to a landform or location.	院 yuàn courtyard 阳 yáng sun
亻	单人旁，一般和人有关系。 The radical “亻” is usually related to a person.	你 nǐ (*singular*) you 他 tā he, him

运用 Application

1 双人活动 Pair Work

两人一组，用“现在……点……分”说说下面的时间。

Work in pairs and talk about the following times using the structure “现在……点……分”.

　　　　Xiànzài jǐ diǎn?
例如：A: 现在 几 点？
　　　　Xiànzài bā diǎn shíbā fēn.
　　　B: 现在 八 点 十八 分。

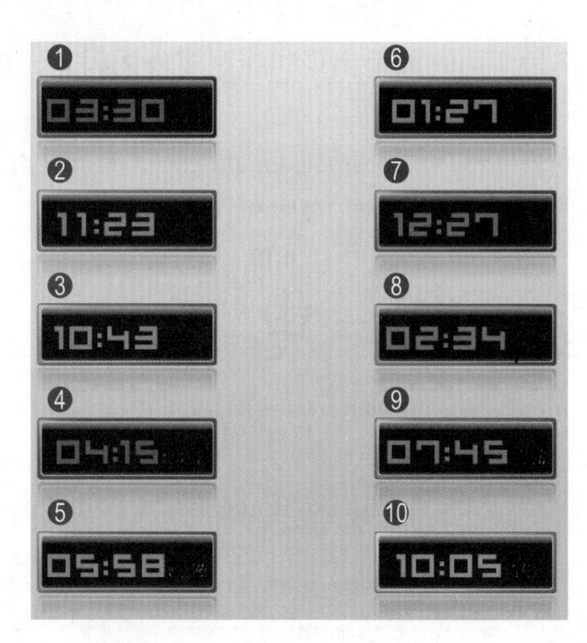

2 小组活动 Group Work

3~4人一组，互相询问并记录一日作息习惯，每组请一位同学报告情况。

Work in groups of 3-4. Ask about each other's daily routines and take notes. Each group chooses one member to make a report.

　　　　Nǐ jǐ diǎn chī zǎofàn?
例如：A: 你 几 点 吃 早饭？
　　　　Wǒ qī diǎn chī zǎofàn.
　　　B: 我 七 点 吃 早饭。

	小王 Xiǎo Wáng			
吃早饭 chī zǎofàn	7:00			
来学校 lái xuéxiào	8:20			
看书 kàn shū	15:00			
回家 huí jiā	18:00 前 (qián)			
看电视 kàn diànshì	晚上 (wǎnshang) 20:00			

12 Míngtiān tiānqì zěnmeyàng 明天天气怎么样 What will the weather be like tomorrow

热身 Warm-up

给下面的词语选择对应的图片

Match the pictures with the words/phrases.

A

B

C

D
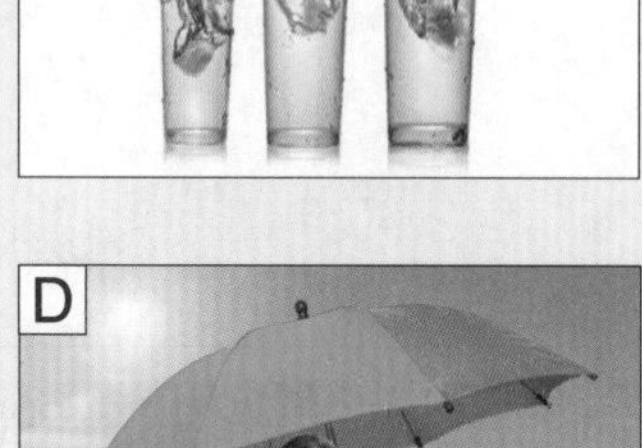

E

F

lěng ① 冷________	rè ② 热________	xià yǔ ③ 下雨________
shuǐ ④ 水________	shuǐguǒ ⑤ 水果________	yīshēng ⑥ 医生________

课文 Text

1 在路上 On the road 12-1

Zuótiān Běijīng de tiānqì zěnmeyàng?
A: 昨天 北京 的天气 怎么样?

Tài rè le.
B: 太热了。

Míngtiān ne? Míngtiān tiānqì zěnmeyàng?
A: 明天 呢? 明天 天气 怎么样?

Míngtiān tiānqì hěn hǎo, bù lěng bú rè.
B: 明天 天气很 好，不 冷 不热。

English Version

A: How was the weather in Beijing yesterday?

B: It was too hot.

A: What about tomorrow? What will the weather be like tomorrow?

B: It will be fine, neither cold nor hot.

New Words

1. 天气 tiānqì n. weather
2. 怎么样 zěnmeyàng pron. (*indicating nature, condition or manner*) how
3. 太 tài adv. too, excessively
   太……了 tài……le too, extremely
4. 热 rè adj. hot
5. 冷 lěng adj. cold

2 在健身房 In the gym 12-2

Jīntiān huì xià yǔ ma?
A: 今天 会 下雨 吗?
Jīntiān bú huì xià yǔ.
B: 今天 不 会下雨。
Wáng xiǎojiě jīntiān huì lái ma?
A: 王 小姐 今天会来吗?
Bú huì lái, tiānqì tài lěng le.
B: 不会来，天气太冷了。

English Version

A: Will it rain today?
B: No, it won't rain.
A: Will Miss Wang come today?
B: No, she won't. It's too cold.

New Words

6. 下雨 xià yǔ to rain
下 xià v. (of rain, snow, etc.) to fall
雨 yǔ n. rain
7. 小姐 xiǎojiě n. miss, young lady
8. 来 lái v. to come

3 在病房 In the sickroom 12-3

Nǐ shēntǐ zěnmeyàng?
A: 你身体 怎么样?
Wǒ shēntǐ bú tài hǎo. Tiānqì tài rè le,
B: 我 身体不太好。天气太热了，
bú ài chī fàn.
不爱吃饭。
Nǐ duō chī xiē shuǐguǒ, duō hē shuǐ.
A: 你多 吃 些 水果，多 喝 水。
Xièxie nǐ, yīshēng.
B: 谢谢 你，医生。

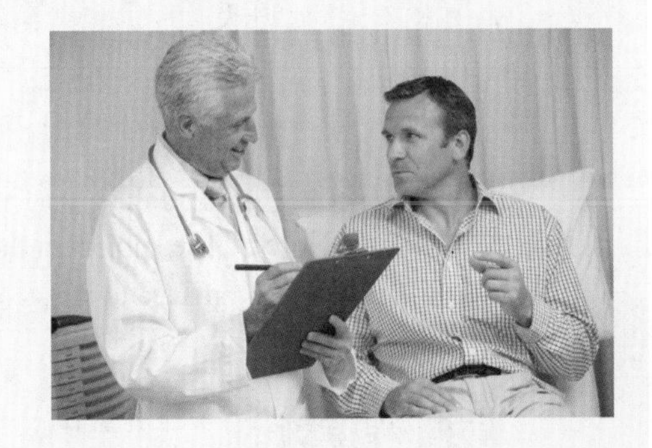

English Version

A: How are you?
B: Not very well. It's too hot. I have no appetite.
A: Eat more fruit and drink more water.
B: Thank you, doctor.

New Words

9. 身体 shēntǐ n. body
10. 爱 ài v. to like, to love
11. 些 xiē m. some, a few
12. 水果 shuǐguǒ n. fruit
13. 水 shuǐ n. water

注释 Notes

1 疑问代词“怎么样” The Interrogative Pronoun “怎么样”

“怎么样”用来询问状况。例如：

“怎么样” is used to ask about the condition of something or someone. For example:

（1）你的汉语怎么样？

（2）你妈妈身体怎么样？

（3）明天天气怎么样？

2 主谓谓语句 Sentences with a Subject-Predicate Phrase as the Predicate

主谓谓语句中的谓语是一个主谓结构的短语，它的格式是：

In Chinese, there is such a kind of sentence in which the predicate is a subject-predicate phrase. The structure is:

全句主语+全句谓语
（主语+谓语）

Subject of the Sentence + Predicate of the Sentence
(Subject + Predicate)

Subject	Predicate	
	Subject	Predicate
我	身体	不太好。
明天	天气	很好。
你	身体	怎么样？

*注意：全句谓语中的主语常常是全句主语的一部分或者跟它相关。

Note: The subject in the subject-predicate phrase is usually part of the subject of the sentence or related to it.

3 程度副词“太” The Adverb “太”

副词“太”表示程度深的意义。用“太”的句尾常带“了”。否定句不用“了”。例如：

The adverb “太” indicates a high degree. “了” is often used at the end of the sentences with “太”, but not in negative sentences. For example:

（1）太热了。

（2）天气太冷了。

（3）我身体不太好。

4 能愿动词"会"（2） The Modal Verb "会" (2)

"会"在句中表示所说的情况有可能实现。例如：

"会" indicates the possibility of the situation mentioned. For example:

（1）A: 爸爸八点前会回家吗？

B: 会。

（2）A: 明天她会来吗？

B: 她会来。

（3）A: 今天会下雨吗？

B: 今天不会下雨。

练习 Exercises

1 分角色朗读课文 Role-play the dialogues.

2 根据课文内容回答问题 Answer the questions based on the dialogues.

1. 昨天北京的天气怎么样？ Zuótiān Běijīng de tiānqì zěnmeyàng?
2. 明天天气怎么样？ Míngtiān tiānqì zěnmeyàng?
3. 今天会下雨吗？ Jīntiān huì xià yǔ ma?
4. 王小姐会来吗？ Wáng Xiǎojiě huì lái ma?
5. 他的身体怎么样？ Tā de shēntǐ zěnmeyàng?

3 用本课新学的语言点和词语描述图片

Describe the pictures using the newly-learned language points and words.

Māma bú tài hǎo.
妈妈_______不太好。

Míngtiān tiānqì hěn hǎo, bú huì
明天天气很好，不会_______。

Wáng Xiǎojiě ài chī
王　小姐 爱 吃________，
bú ài chī fàn.
不爱吃 饭。

Jīntiān tiānqì　　　　nǐ duō hē shuǐ.
今天 天气________，你 多 喝 水。

拼音 Pinyin

三音节词语的声调搭配（1）：一声音节开头 12-4
Tone Collocation in Trisyllabic Words (1): words starting with a first-tone syllable

1+1+1	1+1+2	1+1+3	1+1+4
xīngqī yī Monday	bīngjīlíng ice-cream	xīngqī wǔ Friday	xīngqī liù Saturday
1+2+1	**1+2+2**	**1+2+3**	**1+2+4**
qīngjiégōng cleaner	zhuōmícáng to hide and seek	chī píngguǒ to eat an apple	Jiānádà Canada
1+3+1	**1+3+2**	**1+3+3**	**1+3+4**
gāojiǎobēi goblet	duī xuěrén to make a snowman	huā yǔsǎn colorful umbrella	chī mǐfàn to eat rice
1+4+1	**1+4+2**	**1+4+3**	**1+4+4**
hāmìguā Hami melon	jīqìrén robot	bōlànggǔ rattle-drum	yīwùshì medical room

汉字 Characters

1 认识独体字 Single-Component Characters

（1）"天"，本义表示头顶，后借指"天空"，与"地"相对。

"天" originally meant "the top of the head". It later means "sky", opposite to "地 (earth) ".

tiān

→ → → 天

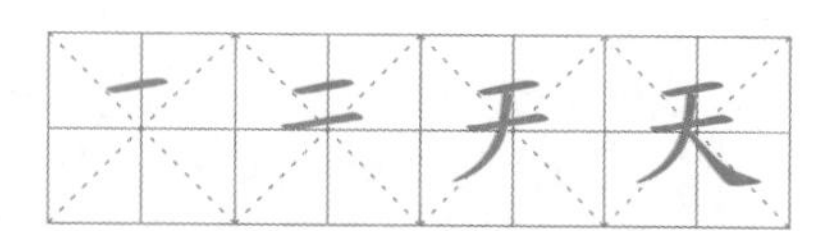

（2）“气”，字形与“三”相似，意思是没有一定的形状、体积，能自由散布的气体。

Shaped like “三”, “气” refers to the air, which has no shape or size and can spread freely.

qì

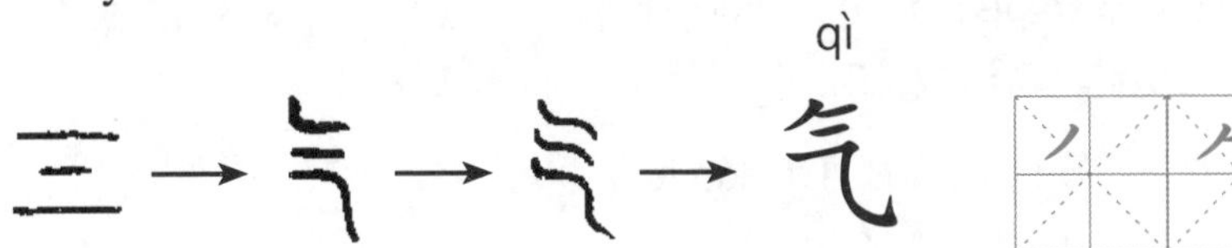

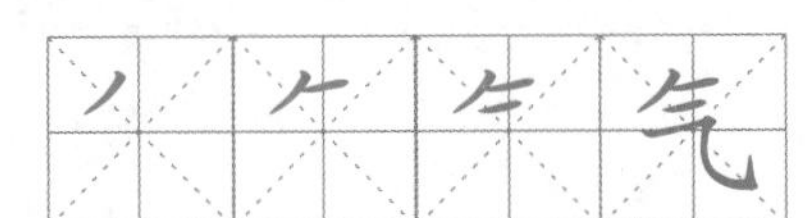

（3）“雨”，字形像从天上降落下来的水滴，表示一种自然现象。

“雨” is shaped like raindrops falling from the sky, indicating the natural phenomenon–“rain”.

yǔ

2 汉字偏旁“女”和“饣” Chinese Radicals: “女” and “饣”

偏旁 Radical	解释 Explanation	例字 Example Characters
女	女字旁，一般和女性有关系。 The radical “女” is usually related to women.	姐 jiě elder sister 妈 mā mother
饣	食字旁，一般和食物有关。 The radical “饣” is usually related to food.	饭 fàn meal 饮 yǐn to drink

运用 Application

1 双人活动 Pair Work

两人一组，用"太……了"做出评价。

Work in pairs and make comments using "太……了" or its negative form.

例如：A: Tā de Hànyǔ zěnmeyàng?
她的 汉语 怎么样？

B: Bú tài hǎo / Tài hǎo le.
不太好 / 太好了。

Běijīng de tiānqì 北京 的天气	lěng rè 冷 热
Zhōngguó cài 中国 菜	hǎochī 好吃
nàge diànyǐng 那个 电影	hǎokàn 好看
Wáng lǎoshī xiě de Hànzì 王 老师 写的 汉字	hǎo 好

2 小组活动 Group Work

3~4人一组，互相询问并记录不同城市最近几天的天气情况，每组请一位同学报告情况。

Work in groups of 3-4. Ask each other about the recent weather conditions in different cities and take notes. Each group chooses one member to make a report.

例如：A: Zuótiān Běijīng tiānqì hǎo ma?
昨天 北京 天气好 吗？

B: Zuótiān hěn hǎo. Bù lěng bú rè.
昨天 很 好。不冷 不热。

A: Míngtiān huì xià yǔ ma?
明天 会下雨吗？

B: Míngtiān bú huì xià yǔ.
明天 不会下雨。

	地名 Place	昨天天气 Yesterday's Weather	今天天气 Today's Weather	明天天气 Tomorrow's Weather
1	北京 Běijīng	很好 hěn hǎo	不太好 bú tài hǎo	不好，很冷 bù hǎo, hěn lěng

13 Tā zài xué zuò Zhōngguó cài ne 他在学做中国菜呢 He is learning to cook Chinese food

热身 Warm-up

给下面的词语选择对应的图片
Match the pictures with the words/phrases.

kàn diànshì ① 看 电视 ________	kàn shū ② 看 书 ________	shuì jiào ③ 睡 觉 ________
dǎ diànhuà ④ 打 电话 ________	zuò fàn ⑤ 做 饭 ________	xuéxí ⑥ 学习 ________

课文 Text

1 打电话 On the phone 13-1

Wèi, nǐ zài zuò shénme ne?
A: 喂，你在做 什么 呢？

Wǒ zài kàn shū ne.
B: 我 在看 书 呢。

Dàwèi yě zài kàn shū ma?
A: 大卫 也 在 看 书 吗？

Tā méi kàn shū, tā zài xué zuò Zhōngguó cài ne.
B: 他 没 看 书，他在 学 做 中国 菜呢。

English Version

A: Hello, what are you doing?
B: I'm reading.
A: Is David reading too?
B: No, he isn't. He is learning to cook Chinese food.

New Words

1. 喂 wèi int. hello, hey
*2. 也 yě adv. also, too
3. 学习（学） xuéxí (xué) v. to study, to learn

Proper Noun

大卫 Dàwèi David

2 在咖啡馆儿 In a coffee house 13-2

Zuótiān shàngwǔ nǐ zài zuò shénme ne?
A: 昨天 上午 你在做 什么 呢?

Wǒ zài shuì jiào ne. Nǐ ne?
B: 我 在 睡 觉 呢。你呢?

Wǒ zài jiā kàn diànshì ne. Nǐ xǐhuan kàn diànshì ma?
A: 我在家看 电视 呢。你 喜欢 看 电视 吗?

Wǒ bù xǐhuan kàn diànshì, wǒ xǐhuan kàn diànyǐng.
B: 我不喜欢 看 电视, 我喜欢 看 电影。

English Version

A: What were you doing yesterday morning?
B: I was sleeping. What about you?
A: I was watching TV at home. Do you like watching TV?
B: No, I don't. I like seeing movies.

New Words

4. 上午 shàngwǔ n. morning, before noon
5. 睡觉 shuì jiào v. to sleep
6. 电视 diànshì n. television
7. 喜欢 xǐhuan v. to like, to be fond of

3 在学校办公室 In the school office 13-3

Bā èr sān líng sì yāo wǔ wǔ, zhè shì Lǐ lǎoshī de diànhuà ma?
A: 82304155, 这是李老师的 电话 吗?

Bú shì. Tā de diànhuà shì bā èr sān líng sì yāo wǔ liù.
B: 不是。她的 电话 是 82304156。

Hǎo, wǒ xiànzài gěi tā dǎ diànhuà.
A: 好, 我 现在 给她打 电话。

Tā zài gōngzuò ne, nǐ xiàwǔ dǎ ba.
B: 她在 工作 呢, 你下午 打吧。

English Version

A: 82304155. Is that Ms. Li's telephone number?
B: No. Her number is 82304156.
A: OK. I'll call her right now.
B: She is working. Call her in the afternoon.

New Words

* 8. 给 gěi prep. to
9. 打电话 dǎ diànhuà to make a phone call
* 10. 吧 ba part. *a modal particle used at the end of a sentence to indicate consultation, a suggestion, request or command*

注释 Notes

1 叹词"喂" The Interjection "喂"

给某人打电话或者接听别人电话开头时的常用语。例如：

The word is often used when calling someone or answering a phone call. For example:

（1）A: 喂，李老师在家吗？
　　B: 她不在家，去学校了。

（2）A: 喂，你是张小姐吗？
　　B: 对，您是？

（3）A: 喂，你在做什么呢？
　　B: 我在看书呢。

2 "在……呢"表示动作正在进行

"在……呢" Used to Indicate an Action in Progress

动词前边加上副词"在"，或者句末用语气助词"呢"表示动作正在进行。例如：

An action in progress can be expressed by adding the adverb "在" before a verb or by using the modal particle "呢" at the end of a sentence. For example:

	在	Verb+Object	（呢）
我	在	睡觉	呢。
你	在	做什么	呢？
小王	在	学习汉语。	

没（在）+ 动词 / 动词词组 表示否定，句尾不能用"呢"。例如：

The negative form is "没（在） + Verb/Verb Phrase", without "呢" at the end of the sentence. For example:

Subject	Predicate	
	没（在）	Verb / Verb Phrase
我	没在	看电视。
他们	没在	工作。
他	没	看书。

3 电话号码的表达 Expression of Telephone Numbers

电话号码的读法与一般数字的读法有所不同。电话号码要一位一位地读。号码中的数字"1"要读成"yāo"。例如：

Telephone numbers are read in a different way than general numbers. They are read digit by digit. The number "1" in a telephone number is read "yāo". For example:

（1）8069478　bā líng liù jiǔ sì qī bā

（2）13851897623　yāo sān bā wǔ yāo bā jiǔ qī liù èr sān

（3）82304156　bā èr sān líng sì yāo wǔ liù

4 语气助词"吧" The Modal Particle "吧"

语气助词"吧"用在祈使句末尾，表示建议或者命令别人，使语气缓和。例如：

When used at the end of an imperative sentence, the modal particle "吧" indicates a suggestion or command with a softened mood. For example:

（1）A: 这儿没有人，请坐吧。
　　 B: 谢谢。

（2）A: 今天我们在家吃饭吧。
　　 B: 好。

（3）A: 我现在给她打电话。
　　 B: 她在工作呢，你下午打吧。

练习 Exercises

1 分角色朗读课文 Role-play the dialogues.

2 根据课文内容回答问题 Answer the questions based on the dialogues.

1. 大卫在做什么呢？ Dàwèi zài zuò shénme ne?
2. 昨天上午他在看书吗？ Zuótiān shàngwǔ tā zài kàn shū ma?
3. 他们都喜欢看电视吗？ Tāmen dōu xǐhuan kàn diànshì ma?
4. 李老师的电话号码是多少？ Lǐ lǎoshī de diànhuà hàomǎ shì duōshao?
5. 李老师在做什么呢？ Lǐ lǎoshī zài zuò shénme ne?

3 用本课新学的语言点和词语描述图片

Describe the pictures using the newly-learned language points and words.

Ānni zài ne.
安妮（Anne）在________呢。

Māma zài
妈妈 在________。

Tā méi kàn shū, zài
他 没 看 书，在________。

Tā méi gōngzuò, ne.
她 没 工作，________呢。

拼音 Pinyin

三音节词语的声调搭配（2）：二声音节开头 13-4

Tone Collocation in Trisyllabic Words (2): words starting with a second-tone syllable

2+1+1	2+1+2	2+1+3	2+1+4
yánjiūshēng postgraduate	tán gāngqín to play the piano	túshūguǎn library	wéishēngsù vitamin
2+2+1	2+2+2	2+2+3	2+2+4
yínhángjiā banker	Hánguó rén Korean (people)	Hánguó yǔ Korean (language)	rénmínbì RMB
2+3+1	2+3+2	2+3+3	2+3+4
yóuyǒngyī swimming suit	yóuyǒngchí swimming pool	yóuyǒngguǎn natatorium	niúzǎikù jean
2+4+1	2+4+2	2+4+3	2+4+4
móshùshī magician	fúwùyuán waiter, waitress	bówùguǎn museum	míngxìnpiàn postcard

汉字 Characters

1 认识独体字 Single-Component Characters

（1）“日”是太阳的形象，本义是太阳。

The character “日” uses the image of the sun and its basic meaning is “the sun”.

rì

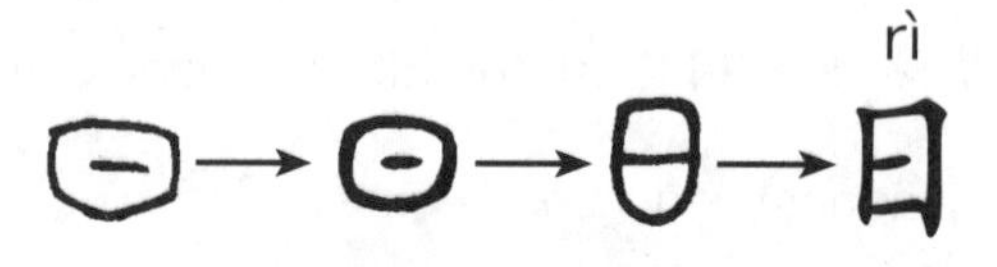

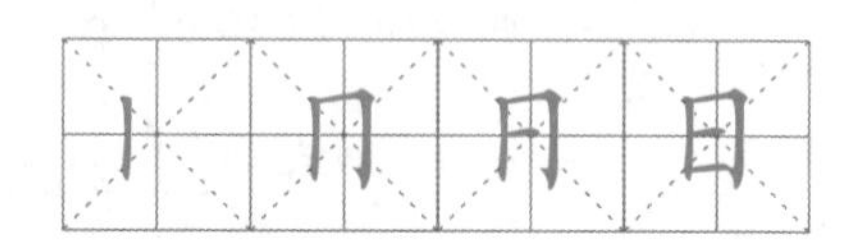

（2）“目”是眼睛的形象，本义是眼睛。

The character “目” uses the image of an eye and its basic meaning is “eye”.

mù

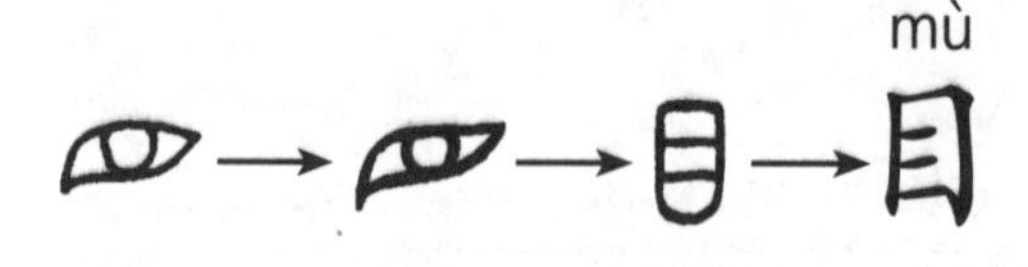

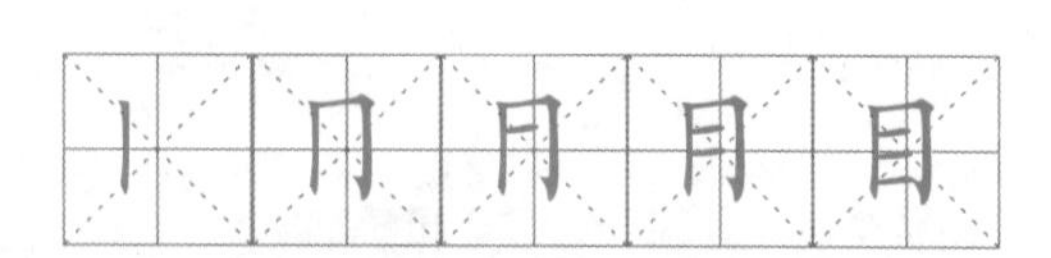

（3）“习”，本义是“学”过后再反复地温习，达到熟练的程度，现在“学”和“习”没什么差异。

The original meaning of “习” was to learn and repeatedly review to achieve proficiency. In modern Chinese, however, it means pretty much the same as “学 (to study/learn)”.

xí

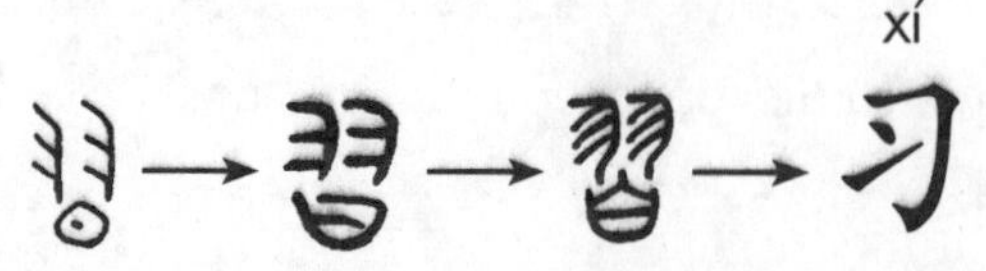

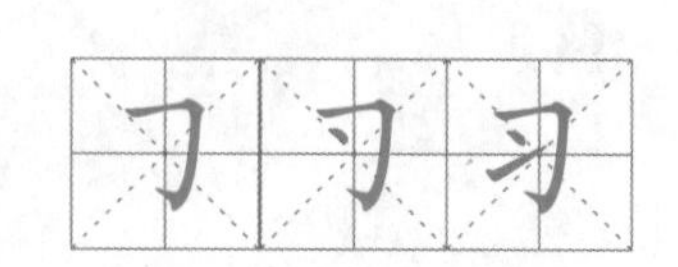

2 汉字偏旁“日”和“目” The Chinese Radicals “日” and “目”

偏旁 Radical	解释 Explanation	例字 Example Characters
日	日字旁，一般和时间有关系。 The radical “日” is usually related to time.	明 míng next 时 shí time
目	目字旁，一般和眼睛有关系。 The radical “目” is usually related to the eyes.	眼 yǎn eye 睡 shuì to sleep

运用 Application

1 双人活动 Pair Work

两人一组，用“昨天……点，我在……（呢）”说说自己昨天的活动。

Work in pairs and talk about what you did yesterday using the pattern “昨天……点，我在……（呢）”.

Zuótiān xiàwǔ wǔ diǎn, nǐ zài zuò shénme ne?

例如：A: 昨天下午五点，你在做什么呢？

Zuótiān xiàwǔ wǔ diǎn, wǒ zài xuéxí ne.

B: 昨天下午五点，我在学习呢。

chī fàn	mǎi dōngxi	kàn diànshì	dǎ diànhuà	shuì jiào
吃饭	买东西	看电视	打电话	睡觉

2 小组活动 Group Work

3~4人一组，互相询问电话号码并记录，每组请一位同学报告情况。

Work in groups of 3-4. Ask each other's telephone numbers and take notes. Each group chooses one member to make a report.

	姓名 Name	电话 Phone Number
1	小王 Xiǎo Wáng	139-0135-1290

14 Tā mǎile bù shǎo yīfu 她买了不少衣服

She has bought quite a few clothes

热身 Warm-up

给下面的词语选择对应的图片

Match the pictures with the words/phrases.

píngguǒ ① 苹果＿＿＿＿＿	chē ② 车＿＿＿＿＿	yīfu ③ 衣服＿＿＿＿＿
shāngdiàn ④ 商店＿＿＿＿＿	shūdiàn ⑤ 书店＿＿＿＿＿	Yīngyǔ shū ⑥ 英语 书＿＿＿＿＿

课文 Text

1 在宿舍 In the dorm

 14-1

Zuótiān shàngwǔ nǐ qù nǎr le?

A: 昨天 上午 你去哪儿了？

Wǒ qù shāngdiàn mǎi dōngxi le.

B: 我 去 商店 买 东西 了。

Nǐ mǎi shénme le?

A: 你买 什么 了？

Wǒ mǎile yìdiǎnr píngguǒ.

B: 我 买了一点儿苹果。

English Version

A: Where did you go yesterday morning?

B: I went shopping.

A: What did you buy?

B: I bought some apples.

New Words

1. 东西 dōngxi n. thing, stuff
2. 一点儿 yìdiǎnr num.-m. a few, a little
3. 苹果 píngguǒ n. apple

2 在公司 In the company 14-2

Nǐ kànjiàn Zhāng xiānsheng le ma?
A: 你看见 张 先生 了吗?
Kànjiàn le, tā qù xué kāi chē le.
B: 看见了，他去学开车了。
Tā shénme shíhou néng huílai?
A: 他什么时候 能 回来?
Sìshí fēnzhōng hòu huílai.
B: 40 分钟 后回来。

English Version

A: Have you seen Mr. Zhang?
B: Yes. He has gone to a driving lesson.
A: When can he come back?
B: After 40 minutes.

New Words

4. 看见 kànjiàn v. to see
5. 先生 xiānsheng n. Mr., sir
6. 开 kāi v. to drive
7. 车 chē n. car, vehicle
8. 回来 huílai v. to come back
9. 分钟 fēnzhōng n. minute
10. 后 hòu n. after, afterwards, later

Proper Noun

张 Zhāng Zhang, a Chinese family name

3 在商店门口 Outside a store 14-3

Wáng Fāng de yīfu tài piàoliang le.
A: 王 方 的衣服太 漂亮 了!
Shì a, tā mǎile bùshǎo yīfu.
B: 是啊，她买了 不少衣服。
Nǐ mǎi shénme le?
A: 你买 什么了?
Wǒ méi mǎi, zhèxiē dōu shì Wáng Fāng de dōngxi.
B: 我 没买，这些都是 王 方 的东西。

English Version

A: Wang Fang's dress is so pretty!
B: Yes. She has bought quite a few clothes.
A: What did you buy?
B: I bought nothing. All these are Wang Fang's stuff.

New Words

11. 衣服 yīfu n. clothes
12. 漂亮 piàoliang adj. beautiful, pretty
*13. 啊 a part. *a modal particle used at the end of a sentence as a sign of confirmation or defense*
14. 少 shǎo adj. little, few
    不少 bùshǎo adj. quite a few, many
15. 这些 zhèxiē pron. these
16. 都 dōu adv. both, all

注释 Notes

1 "了"表发生或完成 "了" Indicating Occurrence or Completion

"了"用于句尾。例如：

"了" can be used at the end of a sentence. For example:

Subject	Predicate	了
我	去商店	了。
他	去学开车	了。
你	买什么	了？

"了"用于动词后带宾语。动词后的宾语前面一般要有定语，如数量词或形容词、代词等。例如：

"了" can also be used between a verb and its object. There is usually a modifier before the object of the verb, such as a numeral classifier, an adjective or a pronoun, etc. For example:

Subject	Predicate			
	Verb	了	Number-Measure Word/ Adjective/Pronoun	Object
她	买	了	一点儿	苹果。
我	买	了	不少	衣服。
你	看见	了	几个	人？

上述两种用法的"了"的否定形式是：没＋动词（＋宾语），"了"要去掉。例如：

The negative form of "了" in both cases above is "没 + verb + (object)". In the negative form, "了" should be omitted. For example:

Subject	没	Predicate
她	没	去商店。
我	没	买。
我	没	看见张先生。

2 名词"后" The Noun "后"

名词"后"表示现在或者所说的某个时间以后的时间。例如：

The noun "后" indicates a period after the present time or the time being mentioned. For example:

（1）五点后　40分钟后　星期三后

（2）A: 你几点去工作？

　　B: 八点后。

（3）A: 你什么时候回家？

　　B: 五点后。

（4）A: 他什么时候能回来？

　　B: 40分钟后回来。

3 语气助词"啊" The Modal Particle "啊"

语气词"啊"用在陈述句末，使句子带上一层感情色彩。"啊"常受到前一字尾音的影响而发生不同的变音，书面上有时按变音写成不同的字。

The modal particle "啊" is used at the end of a declarative sentence to set the mood. The pronunciation of "啊" varies with the finals of the syllables before it, and in written Chinese, the variants are represented by different characters sometimes.

The Final of the Syllable before It	The Pronunciation of "啊"
a　e　i　o　ü	a → ia
u　ao　ou	a → ua
-n	a → na
-ng	a → nga
-i（zi，ci，si 中）	a → za
-i（zhi，chi，shi，ri 中）	a → ra

（1）A: 你是王小姐吗？

　　B: 是啊。

（2）A: 你想去吃中国菜吗？

　　B: 好啊。

（3）A: 王方的衣服太漂亮了！

　　B: 是啊，她买了不少衣服。

4 副词“都” The Adverb “都”

“都”表示总括全部，所总括的对象必须放在“都”的前面。例如：

“都” means “both/all”. The people or objects included are put before “都”. For example:

（1）我们都是中国人。

（2）他们都喜欢喝茶。

（3）这些都是王方的东西。

练习 Exercises

1 分角色朗读课文 Role-play the dialogues.

2 根据课文内容回答问题 Answer the questions based on the dialogues.

1. 昨天上午她去哪儿了？ Zuótiān shàngwǔ tā qù nǎr le?
2. 她买什么了？ Tā mǎi shénme le?
3. 张先生什么时候能回来？ Zhāng xiānsheng shénme shíhou néng huílai?
4. 王方买什么了？ Wáng Fāng mǎi shénme le?
5. 王方的朋友买什么了？ Wáng Fāng de péngyou mǎi shénme le?

3 用本课新学的语言点和词语描述图片

Describe the pictures using the newly-learned language points and words.

Māma qù shāngdiàn mǎile
妈妈去商店买了＿＿＿＿。

Tā xiàwǔ qù xué ＿＿＿＿ le.
她下午去学＿＿＿＿了。

Zhuōzi shang ＿＿＿＿ shì Zhāng xiānsheng de dōngxi.
桌子上＿＿＿＿是张先生的东西。

Lìli mǎile ＿＿＿＿ yīfu.
丽丽买了＿＿＿＿衣服。

拼音 Pinyin

三音节词语的声调搭配（3）：三声音节开头 14-4

Tone Collocation in Trisyllabic Words (3): words starting with a third-tone syllable

3+1+1	3+1+2	3+1+3	3+1+4
xǐyījī washing machine	pǔtōng rén common people	zǒngjīnglǐ general manager	huǒchē piào train ticket
3+2+1	3+2+2	3+2+3	3+2+4
shǐxuéjiā historian	jǐngchájú police station	měinánzǐ handsome man	měiróngyuàn beauty salon
3+3+1	3+3+2	3+3+3	3+3+4
biǎoyǎnjiā performer	xiǎo yǎnyuán little actor	Mǐlǎoshǔ Mickey Mouse	yǎnchànghuì concert
3+4+1	3+4+2	3+4+3	3+4+4
dǎzìjī typewriter	pǎobù xié running shoes	měishùguǎn art gallery	dǎ diànhuà to make a phone call

汉字 Characters

1 认识独体字 Single-Component Characters

（1）“开”，字形像一双手抽拉门栓。本义是抽掉门栓，启动关闭的门，现在意思很多，如“开车”、“开花”。

Shaped like two hands pulling a door latch, the original meaning of “开” was to pull out the door latch and open the door. Now it has many meanings, such as “开车 (to drive a car)” and “开花 (to bloom)”.

kāi

開 → 開 → 开

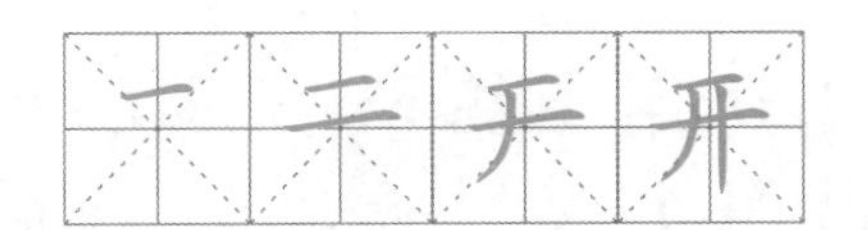

（2）“车”，字形像某种器械两边各有一个轮子，本义是有轮子、靠牛马拉动的战斗工具，现在泛指陆上运输、交通工具，如“出租车”、“火车”。

“车”, originally shaped like an equipment with a wheel on both sides, referred to a wheeled vehicle used in wars, pulled by an ox or a horse. Now it refers to all the vehicles on land for transportation, such as “出租车 (taxi)” and “火车 (train)”.

chē

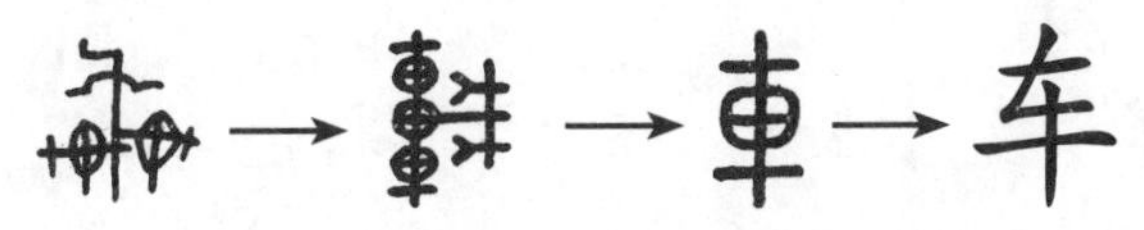

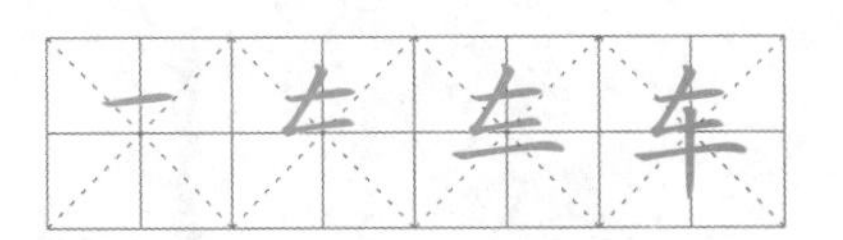

（3）“回”，字形像水流回旋的样子，本义是“旋转”，后来表示“还、回来”。

“回” is shaped like a whirling flow of water. It originally meant “to rotate”, and now it means “to return”.

huí

回

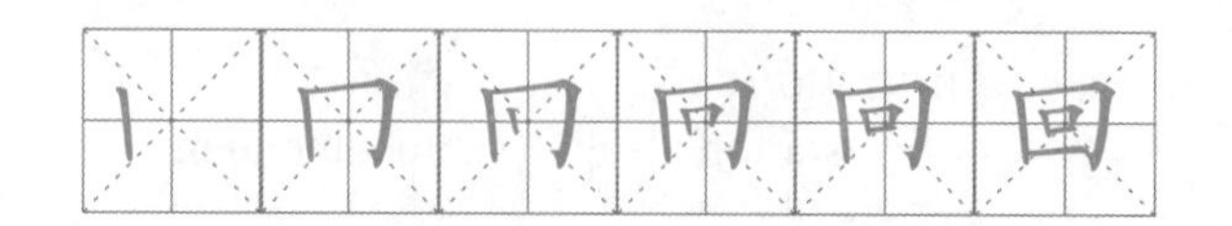

2 汉字偏旁“月”和“扌” Chinese Radicals: “月” and “扌”

偏旁 Radical	解释 Explanation	例字 Example Characters
月	肉月旁，一般和人体、肉有关系。 The radical “月” is usually related to human body or flesh.	服 fú clothes 胖 pàng fat
扌	提手旁，一般表示和手有关的动作。 The radical “扌” usually indicates an action related to a hand.	打 dǎ to beat, to hit 找 zhǎo to look for

运用 Application

1 双人活动 Pair Work

两人一组，询问对方购买的物品。

Work in pairs and ask about the things your partner has bought.

例如：A: Nǐ qù shāngdiàn mǎi shénme le?
你去商店买什么了？

B: Wǒ mǎile……
我买了……

píngguǒ	yīfu	bēizi	zhuōzi	shū
苹果	衣服	杯子	桌子	书

2 小组活动 Group Work

3~4人一组，互相询问并记录小组成员一天的活动，每组请一位同学报告情况。

Work in groups of 3-4. Ask about what each of your group member did during a day in the past and take notes. Each group chooses one member to make a report.

例如：
A: Xīngqī yī shàngwǔ nǐ zuò shénme le?
星期一上午你做什么了？
B: Wǒ qù diànyǐngyuàn le.
我去电影院了。
A: Nǐ kàn shénme le?
你看什么了？
B: Wǒ kànle yí ge Zhōngguó diànyǐng.
我看了一个中国电影。

	人名 Name	时间 Time	地方 Place	做什么 Activity
1	小王 Xiǎo Wáng	星期一上午 xīngqī yī shàngwǔ	电影院 diànyǐngyuàn	看了一个电影 kànle yí ge diànyǐng

15 Wǒ shì zuò fēijī lái de 我是坐飞机来的 I came here by air

热身 Warm-up

给下面的词语选择对应的图片

Match the pictures with the words/phrases.

A 

B 

C 

D 

E 

F 

fēijī ① 飞机 ______	chūzūchē ② 出租车 ______	dàxué ③ 大学 ______
fàndiàn ④ 饭店 ______	tīng ⑤ 听 ______	kāi chē ⑥ 开车 ______

课文 Text

1 在餐桌旁 At the dining table 15-1

Nǐ hé Lǐ xiǎojiě shì shénme shíhou rènshi de?

A：你和李小姐是什么时候认识的？

Wǒmen shì èr líng yī yī nián jiǔ yuè rènshi de.

B：我们是 2011 年 9 月认识的。

Nǐmen zài nǎr rènshi de?

A：你们在哪儿认识的？

Wǒmen shì zài xuéxiào rènshi de, tā shì wǒ dàxué tóngxué.

B：我们是在学校认识的，她是我大学同学。

English Version

A: When did you and Miss Li first meet?

B: We met in September, 2011.

A: Where did you meet each other?

B: We met in our university. She was my classmate.

New Words

1. 认识 rènshi v. to meet, to know
2. 年 nián n. year
3. 大学 dàxué n. college, university

2 在饭店门口 Outside a hotel 15-2

Nǐmen shì zěnme lái fàndiàn de?
A：你们 是 怎么 来 饭店 的？
Wǒmen shì zuò chūzūchē lái de.
B：我们 是 坐 出租车 来 的。
Lǐ xiānsheng ne?
A：李 先生 呢？
Tā shì hé péngyou yìqǐ kāi chē lái de.
B：他 是 和 朋友 一起 开 车 来 的。

English Version

A: How did you come here?
B: We came by taxi.
A: What about Mr. Li?
B: He drove here with his friend.

New Words

4. 饭店 fàndiàn n. hotel, restaurant
5. 出租车 chūzūchē n. taxi, cab
*6. 一起 yìqǐ adv. together

3 在公司 In the company 15-3

Hěn gāoxìng rènshi nín! Lǐ xiǎojiě.
A：很 高兴 认识 您！李 小姐。
Rènshi nǐ wǒ yě hěn gāoxìng!
B：认识 你 我 也 很 高兴！
Tīng Zhāng xiānsheng shuō, nín shì zuò fēijī lái Běijīng de?
A：听 张 先生 说，您 是 坐 飞机 来 北京 的？
Shì de.
B：是 的。

English Version

A: Nice to meet you, Miss Li.
B: Nice to meet you too.
A: Mr. Zhang said you came to Beijing by plane, didn't you?
B: Yes, I did.

New Words

7. 高兴 gāoxìng adj. glad, happy
8. 听 tīng v. to listen
9. 飞机 fēijī n. airplane

注释 Notes

1 “是……的”句：强调时间、地点、方式

The Structure “是……的”: used to emphasize time, place or manner

在已经知道事情发生的情况下，可以用“是……的”强调事情发生的时间、地点、方式等。肯定句和疑问句中的“是”字可以省略，否定句中不能省略。

When the occurrence of something is known, “是……的” can be used to emphasize when, where and in which manner it occurred. “是” can be omitted in positive and interrogative sentences, but not in negative sentences.

Subject	是	Time/Place/Manner	Verb	的
我	是	昨天	来	的。
这	是	在北京	买	的。
你们	是	怎么	来饭店	的？

否定形式：The negative form:

Subject	不	是	Time/Place/Manner	Verb	的
我	不	是	昨天	来	的。
这	不	是	在北京	买	的。
我们	不	是	坐出租车	来	的。

2 日期的表达（2）：年、月、日/号、星期

Expression of a Date (2): year, month, date, day of the week

汉语中日期的写法和读法都是从大到小。年要分别读出每个数字，再加上“年”；月、日要读出整个数字，再加上“月”、“日/号”。星期的读法是“星期”加上数字。如“2008年8月8号，星期五”读法是“èr líng líng bā nián bā yuè bā hào，xīngqī wǔ”。

Chinese dates are written and read from the bigger unit to the smaller. A year is read digit by digit, followed by the character “年”. A month or date is read the whole number followed by “月” and “日/号” respectively. A day of the week is expressed by the word “星期” plus a specific number. For example, “August 8th of 2008, Friday” is read as “èr líng líng bā nián bā yuè bā hào, xīngqī wǔ”.

（1）明天是2014年5月11号。

（2）A: 今天几号？星期几？

B: 今天9月10号，星期三。

（3）我们是2011年9月认识的。

练习 Exercises

1 分角色朗读课文 Role-play the dialogues.

2 根据课文内容回答问题 Answer the questions based on the dialogues.

1. 她们是什么时候认识的？Tāmen shì shénme shíhou rènshi de?
2. 她们是在哪儿认识的？Tāmen shì zài nǎr rènshi de?
3. 他们是怎么去饭店的？Tāmen shì zěnme qù fàndiàn de?
4. 李先生是坐出租车去饭店的吗？
   Lǐ xiānsheng shì zuò chūzūchē qù fàndiàn de ma?
5. 李小姐是怎么来北京的？Lǐ xiǎojiě shì zěnme lái Běijīng de?

3 用本课新学的语言点和词语描述图片

Describe the pictures using the newly-learned language points and words.

Wǒmen shì zài Bālí ________ de.
我们是在巴黎（Paris）________的。

Wǒ méi kànjiàn Lǐ lǎoshī, tā shì shénme shíhou ________?
我没看见李老师，她是什么时候________？

Zhèxiē yīfu bù ________ jīntiān ________ de, shì zuótiān mǎi de.
这些衣服不________今天________的，是昨天买的。

Wǒmen shì yìqǐ ________ lái de, wǒ bù xǐhuan zuò chūzūchē.
我们是一起________来的，我不喜欢坐出租车。

拼音 Pinyin

三音节词语的声调搭配（4）：四声音节开头 15-4

Tone Collocation in Trisyllabic Words (4): words starting with a fourth-tone syllable

4+1+1	4+1+2	4+1+3	4+1+4
diànbīngxiāng refrigerator	Màidāngláo McDonald's	jiànshēnguǎn gym	bàngōngshì office
4+2+1	**4+2+2**	**4+2+3**	**4+2+4**
chàng guógē to sing the national anthem	kàn zúqiú to watch football	kuàngquánshuǐ mineral water	shuànyángròu instant-boiled mutton
4+3+1	**4+3+2**	**4+3+3**	**4+3+4**
mìmǎxiāng code box	qìguǎnyán tracheitis	dàshǐguǎn embassy	mièhuǒqì fire extinguisher
4+4+1	**4+4+2**	**4+4+3**	**4+4+4**
zhàoxiàngjī camera	zànzhùrén sponsor	diànhuàkǎ phone card	Àoyùnhuì Olympic Games

汉字 Characters

1 认识独体字 Single-Component Characters

（1）"年"，本义是将收成的谷物运回家。现在是时间单位。

"年" originally meant "to carry crops home". Now it means "year".

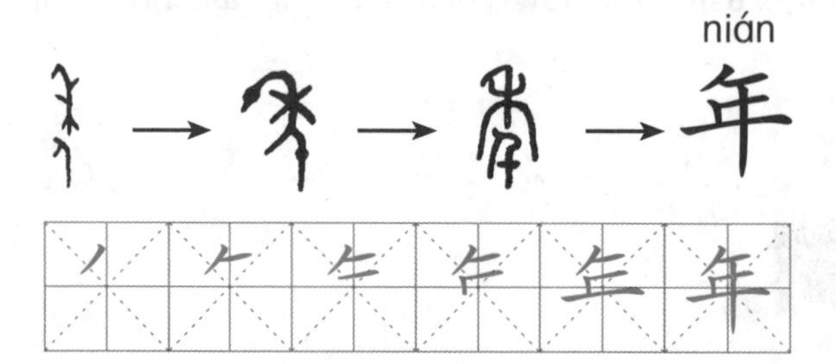

（2）"出"，字形像脚离开某地。现在是从里面到外面的意思。

"出" originally referred to the germination and growth of a plant. Now it means "to come or go from inside to outside".

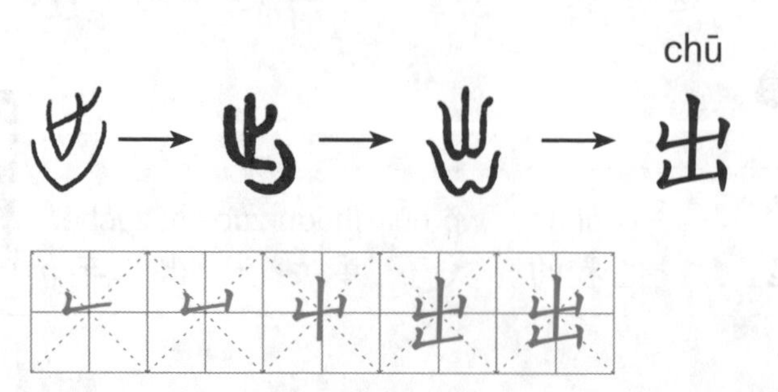

（3）“飞”，本义是鸟类或虫类等用翅膀在空中往来活动，现在泛指在天上飞、快等。

Originally “飞” meant the activity of a bird or an insect flying in the sky with its wings, and now it generally means “to fly in the sky” or “being quick”.

fēi

→ → → 飞

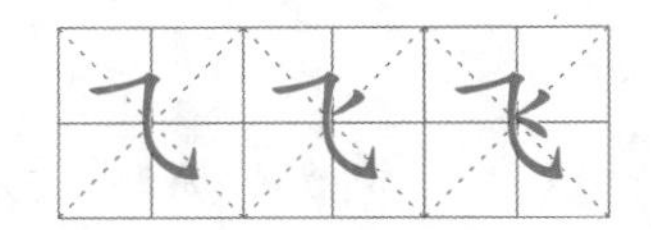

2 汉字偏旁“艹”和“宀” Chinese Radicals: “艹” and “宀”

偏旁 Radical	解释 Explanation	例字 Example Characters
艹	草字头，一般和草木或者植物有关系。 The radical “艹” is usually related to grass, trees or plants.	茶 chá tea 菜 cài vegetable
宀	宝盖头，一般和房子有关系。 The radical “宀” is usually related to houses.	安 ān to settle 家 jiā home

运用 Application

1 双人活动 Pair Work

两人一组，选择对方的一样物品，询问具体购买情况。

Work in pairs and ask each other about where and when something was bought.

例如：A: 这个 是 在哪儿买 的？（Zhège shì zài nǎr mǎi de?）

B: 在 商店 买 的。（Zài shāngdiàn mǎi de.）

A: 什么 时候 买 的？（Shénme shíhou mǎi de?）

B: 昨天 买 的。（Zuótiān mǎi de.）

Hànyǔ shū	yīfu	bēizi	diànnǎo
汉语 书	衣服	杯子	电脑

2 小组活动 Group Work

3~4人一组，互相询问并记录小组各成员会做什么，每组请一位同学报告情况。

Work in groups of 3-4. Ask about the ability of each of your group members and take notes. Each group chooses one member to make a report.

例如：A: Nǐ huì shuō Hànyǔ ma?
你 会 说 汉语 吗？

B: Huì.
会。

A: Nǐ shì shénme shíhou kāishǐ xué Hànyǔ de?
你 是 什么 时候 开始（to start）学 汉语 的？

B: Wǒ shì de.
我 是……的。

A: Nǐ shì zài nǎr xué de?
你 是 在哪儿学 的？

B: Wǒ shì de.
我 是……的。

	姓名 Name	会做什么 Ability	时间 Time	地方 Place
1	小王 Xiǎo Wáng	做中国菜 zuò Zhōngguó cài	今年 jīnnián	北京 Běijīng

文化 CULTURE

中国人经常使用的通信工具
Common Communication Tools of Chinese People

在中国，常用的通信工具有电话机和手机两种。电话机号码一般为7-8位，比如2027816、82304156，不同地区的电话机号码位数不同。手机号码的位数没有地区的差别，都是11位，比如13576983311。由于手机号码位数较多，读时一般切分为“3-4-4”的停顿模式，比如139-0107-8866。其中号码中的“1”要读成“yāo”。

In China, there are two kinds of common communication tools—telephones and cell phones. A telephone number usually has 7-8 digits, for example, 2027816, 82304156. Telephone numbers in different regions have different numbers of digits. Cell phone numbers, however, always have 11 digits regardless of region, as in 13576983311. Since a cell phone number has many digits, it is read with pauses following the pattern “3-4-4”, such as 139-0107-8866. “1” is read as “yāo” in a phone number.

词语总表 Vocabulary

词性对照表 Abbreviations of Parts of Speech

词性 Part of Speech	英文简称 Abbreviation	词性 Part of Speech	英文简称 Abbreviation
名词	n.	副词	adv.
动词	v.	介词	prep.
形容词	adj.	连词	conj.
代词	pron.	助词	part.
数词	num.	叹词	int.
量词	m.	拟声词	onom.
数量词	num.-m.	前缀	pref.
能愿动词	mod.	后缀	suf.

生词 New Words

词语 Word/Phrase	拼音 *Pinyin*	词性 Part of Speech	词义 Meaning	课号 Lesson
			A	
爱	ài	v.	to like, to love	12
			B	
八	bā	num.	eight	5 (notes)
爸爸	bàba	n.	father	9
杯子	bēizi	n.	cup, glass	8
本	běn	m.	*a measure word for books*	10
不客气	bú kèqi		you're welcome, don't mention it	2
不	bù	adv.	no, not	2
			C	
菜	cài	n.	dish, cuisine	6
茶	chá	n.	tea	8
吃	chī	v.	to eat	8
出租车	chūzūchē	n.	taxi, cab	15
			D	
打电话	dǎ diànhuà		to make a phone call	13
大	dà	adj.	(of age) old	5
的	de	part.	*used after an attribute*	4

点	diǎn	m.	o'clock	11
电脑	diànnǎo	n.	computer	10
电视	diànshì	n.	television	13
电影	diànyǐng	n.	film, movie	11
东西	dōngxi	n.	thing, stuff	14
都	dōu	adv.	both, all	14
读	dú	v.	to read	6
对不起	duìbuqǐ	v.	to be sorry	1
多	duō	adv.	*indicating degree or extent*	5
多少	duōshao	pron.	how many, how much	8
E				
儿子	érzi	n.	son	9
二	èr	num.	two	5 (notes)
F				
饭店	fàndiàn	n.	hotel, restaurant	15
飞机	fēijī	n.	airplane	15
分钟	fēnzhōng	n.	minute	14
G				
高兴	gāoxìng	adj.	glad, happy	15
个	gè	m.	*a general measure word*	8
工作	gōngzuò	v./n.	to work; job	9
狗	gǒu	n.	dog	9
H				
汉语	Hànyǔ	n.	Chinese (language)	4
好	hǎo	adj.	good, fine	1
号	hào	n.	(*for date of month*) number	7
喝	hē	v.	to drink	8
和	hé	conj.	and	10
很	hěn	adv.	very, quite	6
后面	hòumiàn	n.	back	10
回	huí	v.	to come/go back, to return	11
会	huì	mod.	can, to be able to	6
J				
几	jǐ	pron.	how many	5
家	jiā	n.	family	5
叫	jiào	v.	to call, to be called	3

今天	jīntiān	n.	today	7
九	jiǔ	num.	nine	5 (notes)
K				
开	kāi	v.	to drive	14
看	kàn	v.	to look at, to watch, to read	7
看见	kàn jiàn	v.	to see	14
块	kuài	m.	*a unit of money, same as "yuan"*	8
L				
来	lái	v.	to come	12
老师	lǎoshī	n.	teacher	3
了	le	part.	*used at the end of or in the middle of a sentence to indicate a change or a new circumstance*	5
冷	lěng	adj.	cold	12
里	li	n.	inner, inside, interior	10
六	liù	num.	six	5 (notes)
M				
妈妈	māma	n.	mother	6
吗	ma	part.	*used at the end of a question*	3
买	mǎi	v.	to buy, to purchase	8
猫	māo	n.	cat	9
没关系	méi guānxi		that's OK, it doesn't matter	1
没有	méiyǒu	adv.	there is not	10
米饭	mǐfàn	n.	cooked rice	8
名字	míngzi	n.	name	3
明天	míngtiān	n.	tomorrow	7
N				
哪	nǎ	pron.	which	4
哪儿	nǎr	pron.	where	9
那	nà	pron.	that	8
呢	ne	part.	*used at the end of a question*	4
能	néng	mod.	can, may	10
你	nǐ	pron.	(*singular*) you	1
年	nián	n.	year	15
女儿	nǚ'ér	n.	daughter	5
P				
朋友	péngyou	n.	friend	4
漂亮	piàoliang	adj.	beautiful, pretty	14

苹果	píngguǒ	n.	apple	14
Q				
七	qī	num.	seven	5 (notes)
前面	qiánmiàn	n.	front	10
钱	qián	n.	money	8
请	qǐng	v.	*(polite)* please	7
去	qù	v.	to go	7
R				
热	rè	adj.	hot	12
人	rén	n.	human, person	3
认识	rènshi	v.	to meet, to know	15
S				
三	sān	num.	three	5 (notes)
商店	shāngdiàn	n.	shop, store	8
上	shang	n.	up, above	10
上午	shàngwǔ	n.	morning, before noon	13
少	shǎo	adj.	little, few	14
谁	shéi	pron.	who, whom	4
什么	shénme	pron.	what	3
十	shí	num.	ten	5 (notes)
时候	shíhou	n.	time, moment	11
是	shì	v.	to be	3
书	shū	n.	book	7
水	shuǐ	n.	water	12
水果	shuǐguǒ	n.	fruit	12
睡觉	shuì jiào	v.	to sleep	13
说	shuō	v.	to speak, to say	6
四	sì	num.	four	5 (notes)
岁	suì	m.	year (of age)	5
T				
他	tā	pron.	he, him	4
她	tā	pron.	she, her	4
太	tài	adv.	too, excessively	12
天气	tiānqì	n.	weather	12
听	tīng	v.	to listen	15
同学	tóngxué	n.	classmate	4

W				
喂	wèi	int.	hello, hey	13
我	wǒ	pron.	I, me	3
我们	wǒmen	pron.	we, us	11
五	wǔ	num.	five	5 (notes)
X				
喜欢	xǐhuan	v.	to like, to be fond of	13
下	xià	n.	under, below	9
下午	xiàwǔ	n.	afternoon	8
下雨	xià yǔ		to rain	12
先生	xiānsheng	n.	Mr., sir	14
现在	xiànzài	n.	now	11
想	xiǎng	mod.	to want, would like	8
小	xiǎo	adj.	small, little	9
小姐	xiǎojiě	n.	miss, young lady	12
些	xiē	m.	some, a few	12
写	xiě	v.	to write	6
谢谢	xièxie	v.	to thank	2
星期	xīngqī	n.	week	7
学生	xuésheng	n.	student	3
学习	xuéxí	v.	to study, to learn	13
学校	xuéxiào	n.	school	7
Y				
一	yī	num.	one	5 (notes)
衣服	yīfu	n.	clothes	14
医生	yīshēng	n.	doctor	9
医院	yīyuàn	n.	hospital	9
椅子	yǐzi	n.	chair	9
一点儿	yìdiǎnr	num.-m.	a few, a little	14
有	yǒu	v.	to have, there be	5
月	yuè	n.	month	7
Z				
再见	zàijiàn	v.	to see you around	2
在	zài	v./prep.	to be in/on/at; in/on/at	9
怎么	zěnme	pron.	(*indicating nature, condition or manner, etc.*) how	6
怎么样	zěnmeyàng	pron.	(*indicating nature, condition or manner*) how	12

这	zhè	pron.	this	8
中午	zhōngwǔ	n.	noon	11
住	zhù	v.	to live, to stay	11
桌子	zhuōzi	n.	desk, table	10
字	zì	n.	character, word	6
昨天	zuótiān	n.	yesterday	7
坐	zuò	v.	to sit, to be seated	10
做	zuò	v.	to make, to produce	6

专有名词 Proper Nouns

词语 Word/Phrase	拼音 *Pinyin*	词义 Meaning	课号 Lesson
		B	
北京	Běijīng	Beijing, capital of China	11
		D	
大卫	Dàwèi	David	13
		L	
李月	Lǐ Yuè	Li Yue, name of a person	3
		M	
美国	Měiguó	the United States of America	3
		W	
王方	Wáng Fāng	Wang Fang, name of a person	10
		X	
谢朋	Xiè Péng	Xie Peng, name of a person	10
		Z	
张	Zhāng	Zhang, a Chinese family name	14
中国	Zhōngguó	China	3

超纲词 Words Not Included in the Syllabus

词语 Word/Phrase	拼音 *Pinyin*	词性 Part of Speech	词义 Meaning	课号 Lesson	级别 Level
			A		
*啊	a	part.	*a modal particle used at the end of a sentence as a sign of confirmation or defense*	14	三级
			B		
*吧	ba	part.	*a modal particle used at the end of a sentence to indicate consultation, a suggestion, request or command*	13	二级

G					
*给	gěi	prep.	to	13	二级
H					
*好吃	hǎochī	adj.	delicious, tasty	6	二级
K					
*口	kǒu	m.	*a measure word for members of families, etc.*	5	三级
N					
*您	nín	pron.	(*polite*) you	1	二级
S					
*身体	shēntǐ	n.	body	12	二级
W					
*问	wèn	v.	to ask, to inquire	7	二级
Y					
*也	yě	adv.	also, too	13	二级
*一起	yìqǐ	adv.	together	15	二级

旧字新词 New Words Made Up of Characters Learned before

来自本册 From This Book

新词 New Word	拼音 *Pinyin*	词性 Part of Speech	词义 Meaning	课号 Lesson	旧字 Learned Characters
B					
不少	bùshǎo	adj.	quite a few, many	14	不、少
C					
车	chē	n.	car, vehicle	14	出租车
吃饭	chī fàn	v.	to eat a meal	11	吃、米饭
D					
大学	dàxué	n.	college, university	15	大、学校
F					
分	fēn	m.	minute	11	分钟
G					
国	guó	n.	country, nation	4	中国
H					
汉字	Hànzì	n.	Chinese character	6	汉语、字
后	hòu	n.	after, afterwards, later	14	后面
回来	huílai	v.	to come back	14	回、起来
J					
今年	jīnnián	n.	this year	5	今天、年

M					
没	méi	adv.	there is not	10	没有
N					
那儿	nàr	pron.	there	9	那、哪儿
你们	nǐmen	pron.	(*plural*) you	1	你、我们
Q					
前	qián	n.	before, earlier than	11	前面
T					
太……了	tài……le		too, excessively	12	太、了
X					
下	xià	v.	(of rain, snow, etc.) to fall	12	下雨
下面	xiàmiàn	n.	under, below	9	下、前面
学	xué	v.	to study, to learn	13	学习
Y					
雨	yǔ	n.	rain	12	下雨
Z					
这儿	zhèr	pron.	here	10	这、哪儿
这些	zhèxiē	pron.	these	14	这、些

补充 Supplementary Vocabulary

新词 New Word	旧字 Learned Characters
茶杯	茶
	杯子
打车	打电话
	出租车
电影院	电影
	医院
汉字	汉语
	字
开车	开
	出租车
里面	里
	前面、后面
明年	明天
	年

新词 New Word	旧字 Learned Characters
朋友们	朋友
	我们
前天	前面
	今天、明天
上面	上
	前面、后面
书店	书
	饭店
说话	说
	打电话
他们	他
	我们
她们	她
	我们

新词 New Word	旧字 Learned Characters
听见	听
	看见
学车	学习
	出租车
学生们	学生
	我们
有点儿	有
	一点儿
这么	这
	什么、怎么
这样	这
	怎么样
做饭	做
	米饭